GUIDE
TO THE
BUDDHIST RUINS OF SARNATH

ARCHAEOLOGICAL SURVEY OF INDIA

GUIDE
TO THE
BUDDHIST RUINS OF SARNATH

WITH SEVEN PLATES

BY

DAYA RAM SAHNI, M.A., RAI BAHADUR,

Director-General of Archaeology in India.

Fifth Edition

GYAN

Published by

Gyan Publishing House
5, Ansari Road
Daryaganj, New Delhi-110002
Phone: 011-47034999, 9811692060
E-mail: books@gyanbooks.com

Distribution Network
gyanbooks.com
India, USA, Canada, UK, Australia, France

ISBN : 978-81-212-2440-6 (HB)
First Published, 1933

2nd Impression 2021

Printed at: Gyan Press, Delhi.

Guide
to the
Buddhist Ruins of Sarnath
Author: Daya Ram Sahni

ARCHÆOLOGICAL SURVEY OF INDIA

GUIDE

TO THE

BUDDHIST RUINS OF SARNATH

WITH SEVEN PLATES

BY

DAYA RAM SAHNI, M.A., RAI BAHADUR,

Director-General of Archæology in India.

FIFTH EDITION

DELHI: MANAGER OF PUBLICATIONS
1933

PREFACE.

THIS little pamphlet is one of a series of Guide-books which the Archæological Survey of India is gradually providing for the use of visitors to places of interest. During the last twenty years, the Archæological Department, under the guidance of Sir John Marshall, has explored a large number of ancient sites that had hitherto lain buried under the ground. The Buddhist site at Sārnāth, four miles north of Benares, possesses a special interest as it was here that after attaining divine wisdom at Gayā, Gautama Buddha preached his first sermon, or. as it is described in the Buddhist sacred texts, began 'to turn the wheel of the good law'. The excavation of the site has not yet been completed, but it is obvious that most of the principal monuments have already been unearthed and a few of these have been identified with tolerable certainty.

The plan that accompanies this handbook has been brought up to date by filling in all the exploration work carried out since the publication of the previous edition, up to the year 1922. The division of the excavated portion of the site into the Stūpa and Monastery areas is no longer sustainable, as it is found that whereas the Main Shrine with its numerous subsidiary structures occupies the central portion, the monasteries are ranged on three sides of it. The text has also been completed and has naturally had to be revised and enlarged in several places. The addition to the introduction of a small chapter on the Benares School of Sculpture will, it is hoped, be appreciated by those visitors who do not care for the detailed information provided in my Catalogue of the Sārnāth Museum. It will be observed that the names of the buildings hitherto described as the Jagat Singh Stūpa and Kittoe's Monastery have been changed to their more appropriate designations. Similarly, my enquiries about the real character of Monastery I lead to the conclusion that this building must be identical with the Dharma-chakra-Jinavihāra erected at Sārnāth by Kumāradevī, queen of Govindachandra of Kanauj.

The route, the visitor is recommended to follow over these remains, is indicated by a red line in the Plan of Excavations. The buildings are described in the same order.

The handbook is based on the accounts of the excavations published in the Annual Reports of the Archæological Survey of India for the years 1904-05, 1906-07, 1907-08 and 1914-15, the valuable summaries contributed by the Director General of Archæology to the Journal of the Royal Asiatic Society and on the descriptions of the work carried out by myself since 1917 in my Annual Progress Reports for the last five years. I have also derived much help from Dr. Vogel's introduction to my Catalogue of the Museum of Archæology at Sārnāth.

DAYA RAM SAHNI.

CAMP KURUKSHETRA,

25th December 1922.

FIFTH EDITION.

The portion of this guide dealing with the Museum has been re-written to conform with the re-arrangement of its contents carried out in 1929-30 under the supervision of Rai Bahadur Ramaprasad Chanda. For the rest it remains unchanged.

15th June 1933. DAYA RAM SAHNI.

GUIDE TO THE BUDDHIST RUINS OF SARNATH.

THE Buddhist remains of Sārnāth are situated some four miles to the north of the city of Benares. In ancient Buddhist texts these remains are called by the name of Rishipatana or Mrigadāva. The first name is explained by the Chinese pilgrim Fa-Hian, who travelled in India in the first half of the 5th century A. D., as meaning "the fall of the sage", *i.e.*, the place where a certain Pratyeka-Buddha, on hearing of the near enlightenment of Gautama Buddha attained *nirvāna*, that is, died. The latter name enshrines a legend which runs as follows* :— In one of his previous existences, Gautama Buddha was the lord of a herd of deer which roamed a large forest where Sārnāth is now situated. His cousin Devadatta was the king of another herd of deer in the same forest. At this time, the king of Benares wandered about hunting and killing the deer of the forest. The Bodhisattva Gautama Buddha, the king of the deer, approached the king and offered to send a deer each day for his food if he would refrain from such promiscuous destruction of his followers. The king agreed to the proposition and went away home. So each day a deer from the respective flocks was sent to the king. Now, among the herd of Devadatta there was a doe big with young and when her turn came to die, she remonstrated with the Bodhisattva saying that although she was ready to die, it was not humane to kill an unborn child. The Bodhisattva was moved and replied that he would that day take her place and die. So he made for the king's palace and when the latter in great astonishment enquired of him the reason of his coming, the king of the deer told him all about the doe and offered himself in her place. The king of Benares was deeply touched and replied, "I am a deer in human form, you are a man in the shape of a deer". He also directed that the slaughter of the deer should cease immediately and gave up the forest for the free use of the deer. The forest was hence called the Deer-Park. General Cunningham suggests that the modern name Sārnāth is derived from "Sāranganātha" meaning "Lord of the Deer", *i.e.*, Gautama Buddha. It is interesting to observe that Sāranganātha is also an epithet of the Brahmanical deity Siva, and the name is still borne by the little Mahādeva shrine situated half a mile east of the Buddhist remains of Sārnāth. Isipatana was also the scene of one of the 550 Jātakas, *i.e.*, the Udapāna-dūsaka-jātaka, which was told by the Buddha whilst dwelling at Isipatana. A jackal used to foul the well where the Brethren used to draw water, and then to make off. One day he was pelted by the novices and after that he never came to look at the place again. The Master heard the Brethren discussing the matter in the Hall of Truth and remarked that that was not the first time that that jackal had fouled the well. He had done the same thing before. He then narrated the

* See the *Nigrodha Miga-Jātaka* in the *Mahāvatthu*, p. 366

story and concluded it with the remark that he himself was the chief of the ascetic band that resided at Isipatana.

In the inscriptions discovered on the site, the locality is invariably referred to as the Dharmachakra or Saddharma-chakrapravartana-vihāra, *i.e.*, "the monastery of the turning of the wheel of the good law". This event is believed to have taken place in the 35th year of the Buddha's life corresponding to the year 528 B. C. The recipients of the sermon were his five former comrades, Ajnāta-Kaundinya and others, who had kept him company during six long years of his austerities but had deserted him on the eve of his enlightenment. They were soon followed by fifty-five other converts and the Master sent all of them off in different directions with the words, "Go forth, O monks, wandering and preaching." The text of this memorable discourse was supplied by "the four noble truths" (Sanskrit *chatvāri āryasatyāni*) of Buddhism. They are enumerated in a short Pāli inscription, cut on the top of a stone umbrella discovered in 1906-07 by Sir John Marshall in the area to the west of the Main Shrine, and may be rendered as follows :—"Four are, ye monks, the noble truths. And which are these four ? The noble truth about suffering, ye monks, the noble truth about the origin of suffering, the noble truth about the cessation of suffering, and the noble truth about the way leading to the cessation of suffering." This sermon begins with an exhortation to avoid two extremes, namely, habitual devotion, on the one hand, to the passions and pleasures of sexual things and habitual devotion, on the other hand, to self-mortification which are both equally painful and unworthy and unprofitable. The Buddha, says the great Teacher, has discovered a middle path which leads to the destruction of sorrow. It is no other than the Aryan Eightfold Path which consists in Right Views, Right Aspirations, Right Speech, Right Conduct, Right Mode of Livelihood, Right Endeavour, Right Mindfulness and Right Rapture. This first sermon is one of the four principal events of the life of Gautama Buddha, which are his birth at Kapilavastu, his enlightenment near Gayā, his first sermon at Isipatana (modern Sārnāth) and his demise at Kusinārā (modern Kasiā in the Gorakhpur District). The sacred texts of the Buddhists tell us that one of the injunctions, the great Teacher gave to his disciples shortly before his demise, was that they should pay regular visits to the four places referred to above. This commandment has been kept faithfully by the Buddhists from the time of the Buddha to the period when these holy places were involved in ruin and became totally forgotten. The great popularity enjoyed by Sārnāth, the birth-place of the Buddhist doctrine, is eloquently proved by the large abundance of religious buildings and other monuments that were built and rebuilt on this spot during the many centuries of its existence by the four classes of Buddhist votaries, *i.e.*, laymen and laywomen and monks and nuns. The remains of these buildings have now been brought to light by the Archæological Survey of India, and the locality has again become a place of pilgrimage for the Buddhists who visit it in large numbers and have built two monasteries of their own not far from the site*.

Sārnāth is also holy ground to the Jainas, who look upon it as the scene of the asceticism and death of Sri Amsanātha, the thirteenth predecessor of Mahāvīra, the historic founder of Jainism. The modern temple near the Dhamekh Stūpa is dedicated to this saint. It is to be observed, however, that the only Jaina antiquities discovered at the excavations of Sārnāth are a few images of the Jaina patriarchs of the mediæval period. These sculptures must have been brought from elsewhere and put up at Sārnāth when Buddhism was on its decline. The same must have been the case with the 25 Brahmanical sculptures, described in the Catalogue of the Museum of Archæology at Sārnāth and several others, which have since been unearthed among the ruins. The most noteworthy of these is the unfinished colossal statue, in late style, of Mahādeva piercing the demon Tripura with his trident, now placed against the west wall of the Southern gallery of the Museum.

Nothing is known about the history of the Deer-Park during the three centuries that followed the preaching of the first sermon by the Buddha, for no antiquities of that period have yet been found. We may, therefore, suppose that such members of the religious order founded by the great Teacher as settled down at the Deer-Park were content, as were the other hermits of that time, with simple huts composed of branches and leaves of trees (Sanskrit *parna-sālā*). The image of the Buddha had not yet come into existence, and the need for Buddhist shrines had not arisen.

The earliest Buddhist monuments known to exist in India are the relic towers or *stūpas* raised by the Buddhist Emperor Asoka over the corporeal remains of the Master, which he obtained from eight earlier *stūpas* in which these remains had been originally enshrined on his death at Kusinārā (modern Kasiā in the Gorakhpur District). The number of the *stūpas* which the Emperor erected, as a means of paying worship to the relics of the Master, soon after his conversion to Buddhism by his spiritual teacher Upagupta, is stated to have been 84,000, but this is no doubt an exaggeration. Some of the *stūpas* of Asoka were in their turn opened by Kānishka, the Kushān king of Northern India, who re-deposited the relics thus obtained in new *stūpas* of his own. One of these *stūpas* with a casket containing three small pieces of the Buddha's remains was discovered near Peshawar by Dr. D. B. Spooner, O.B.E.,

* The Mahābodhi Society of Calcutta have also erected at Sārnāth a *vihāra* to enshrine certain Buddhist relics found by Sir John Marshall at Taxila which have been presented to them by the Government of India. The ceremony for the laying of the foundation stone of this building was performed by His Excellency Sir Harcourt Butler, Governor of the United Provinces, on the 3rd November 1922 and the building was completed in 1931.

of the Archæological Department, in 1908-09. These relics were presented by the Government of India to the Buddhist community of Burma, where they have been enshrined in a suitable Pagoda at Mandalay. Other monuments of Asoka, besides the partially explored monastery at Piprahwa in the district of Basti, that have come down to us are his magnificent monolithic columns which he erected in the course of a pilgrimage to the Buddhist sacred places about the year B. C. 249, and his celebrated edicts which he had engraved on rocks.

At Sārnāth three Asokan monuments have been unearthed, and these are the earliest and most important relics hitherto found at this site. The Asoka pillar which came to light to the west of the temple referred to in this handbook as the Main Shrine, has suffered irreparable damage and only a small portion of it is now standing in position. On its west face is an edict issued by the Emperor Asoka as a warning to the monks and nuns residing in the Deer-Park against schisms. What necessitated such a step on the part of the august patron of the Buddhist Church at that early stage in its history is not yet definitely known.

The next monument which most probably dates from the time of Asoka is the brick *stūpa* or relic tower situated to the south of the Asoka pillar, generally referred to in the Archæological Survey Reports as the Jagat Singh Stūpa as it was demolished, in 1794 A. D., by Babu Jagat Singh, Diwan of Raja Chet Singh of Benares. The third monument of the same epoch is the monolithic railing which was discovered in 1904-05 under the floor of the south chapel of the Main Shrine. To judge from bas-relief representations of ancient *stūpas* and from similar monuments recently restored at Sānchī by Sir John Marshall, the railing at Sārnāth must have formed the crowning feature of the Jagat Singh *stūpa*, which is undoubtedly a Dharmarājikā of Asoka. To the Sunga period (circa 200 B. C.) belonged a stone railing, some posts and rails of which were found built in the walls of a later structure. The inscriptions engraved on several of these posts show that the cost of the railing was contributed by a number of donors: monks, nuns and lay members. We note that two of these pillars were, in the Gupta period, *i.e.*, the fourth or fifth century A. D., converted into lamp posts for the " principal shrine of the Lord Buddha ". The architectural and other fragments unearthed in 1914-15 by Mr. Hargreaves in the area to the west of the Asoka pillar belong to the same or a somewhat earlier period.

The inscriptions discovered at Sārnāth throw some light on the different sects that have occupied this place. From three of these records we gather that about 300 A. D., the entire establishment was in the hands of the Sarvāstivādi priests of the old or orthodox school of Buddhism. It is also apparent from one of the same three epigraphs that Sārnāth had, before this, been in the possession of another sect, the name of which has not been preserved. That the Sarvāstivādins did not remain in power for a long time is proved by an inscription of the 4th century engraved on the Asoka Pillar by the teachers of another sect, the Sammitiyas, a branch of the orthodox Vātsiputrika sect. The latter had a much longer regime for, when the Chinese pilgrim Hiuen Tsang visited Sārnāth in the 7th century A. D., they still occupied the predominant position at Sārnāth.

The Chinese pilgrims Fa-Hian and Hiuen Tsang, who visited the holy places of the Buddhists in India in the 5th and 7th centuries respectively, have left us valuable information regarding the Deer-Park. The former tells us that in his time the Deer-Park possessed four large topes and two monasteries with monks residing in them. In the time of Hiuen Tsang the Deer-Park was in a much more prosperous condition, and not less than 1,500 priests resided in it. Of the numerous *stūpas* and other religious buildings described by him in his itinerary, the principal-shrines were a magnificent temple containing a life size brass image representing the Buddha as turning the wheel of the law, a stone *stūpa* built by Asoka and a stone pillar erected by the same Emperor. The last two of these have already been referred to. The temple which contained the brass image of the Buddha must evidently have been the same as the principal temple of the Lord referred to above and which should most probably be recognised in the temple now designated as the Main Shrine. Among the later structures only one can be identified with certainty. This is the building which has hitherto been described as Monastery I, but which, there are cogent reasons to believe, must be identified with the temple of the Lord of the Wheel of the Law founded in the first half of the 12th century A. D., by Kumāradevī, queen of king Govindachandra of Kanauj (see p. 28 below).

The monastic settlement of Sārnāth continued in use until the end of the 12th century, when it was devastated in 1194 A. D., by Muhammad Ghorī when his general Qutb-ud-dīn defeated Jai Chand, the Raja of Benares, and destroyed a large number of temples and images. It is obvious, however, that already before their final destruction, these buildings had suffered more than once from wanton destruction at the hands of hostile invaders or from the neglect of the devotees. But on each occasion they were readily renewed by pious votaries who visited the place from all parts of India. The earliest invaders were perhaps the white Huns who under the leadership of the tyrant, Mihirakula, overran the Gangetic plains in the beginning of the 6th century A. D. That the Buddhist buildings of Sārnāth were probably plundered during these invasions receives support from the fact that General Cunningham found a large collection of statues of the 4th or 5th century A. D. packed together in a small room which, he believed, had been hidden away in it on the occasion of one of these invasions.

We possess indirect evidence of another serious attack on these buildings. This is supplied by an interesting dedicatory inscription engraved in Sanskrit on the base of a statue of the Buddha [No. B. (c) 1 in the Sārnāth Museum] which states that the principal monuments of the Deer-Park were restored by two brothers, Sthirapāla and Vasantapāla, in the reign of Mahīpāla, king of Bengal. This took place in the year 1026 A. D., *i.e.*, only nine years after the capture of Benares by Mahmūd of Ghaznī, so that we may assume that this restoration was necessitated by the wholesale devastation carried out at Sārnāth by the great iconoclast.

The pious brothers referred to in the last-mentioned inscription also erected "a new shrine of stone pertaining to the eight great places". The eight places are not defined, and the real character of the shrine is uncertain. Dr. Vogel suggests that the shrine was so called as it contained a sculpture representing the eight main events of the Buddha's life. One such sculpture, though of an earlier period, was indeed discovered at Sārnāth and is noticed in the sequel. *

The restoration carried out by the Pāla brothers must have been of a lasting character. The principal buildings of Sārnāth were existing in good condition in the year 1058 A. D., and in the first half of the 12th century A. D., the Queen Kumāradevī, referred to above, restored the image of the Buddha in the act of turning the wheel of the law. The inscription recording this pious act makes the image of the Buddha referred to as old as the time of Asoka but this was, no doubt, due to a misconception, as images of the Buddha were unknown at that early date.

It has been stated above, that the final destruction of the Sārnāth buildings was presumably the work of Muhammad Ghorī, and the condition of the remains that have now been unearthed shows clearly that their overthrow was due to a violent catastrophe accompanied with plunder and fire. What portions remained of these buildings were soon buried under their own débris and dust so that the only structures that remained above the surface were the large *stūpa* locally known as the Dhamekh *stūpa* and another large *stūpa* mound which was destroyed by Jagat Singh. A third Buddhist monument that survived was the mound called by the villagers the Chaukhandī, which is situated at a distance of half-a-mile from the main site of the Deer-Park.

History of Exploration.

The Deer-Park ceased to exist as a place of worship and fell completely into oblivion until an accidental discovery at the end of the 18th century A. D., drew the attention of the European officers of Benares to its great antiquarian importance and led the way to its exploration

* No. C (a) 3 on p. 45.

by archæologists. This discovery was made in the year 1794 A. D. by the workmen of Babu Jagat Singh, Diwan of Chait Singh, the Raja of Benares, when they were dismantling one of the monuments of Sārnāth, to obtain bricks for the construction of a market place in Benares which is still known as Jagat Ganj. The relics discovered on this occasion created a widespread interest in the ruins of Sārnāth. The earliest excavations, of which we are aware, were carried out in 1815 A. D., when Colonel C. Mackenzie examined some of these remains, and presented the sculptures found by him to the Asiatic Society of Bengal. They are now in the Indian Museum, Calcutta, but no account of his explorations seems to have been published. General Sir Alexander Cunningham, the first Director General of Archæology in India, carried out valuable excavations at this site at his own expense from December 1834 to January 1836. He opened the Dhamekh Stūpa and the Chaukhandī mound and exposed a mediæval monastery and a temple to the north of the Jagat Singh Stūpa. He also unearthed a collection of statues which may be seen in the Indian Museum, Calcutta. Some forty sculptures and numerous carved stones were left by General Cunningham at Sārnāth. Some of these were used up in the construction of two bridges on the river Barnā as appears from the following passage in the Reverend Mr. Sherring's book, The Sacred City of the Hindus, which tells us that " in the erection of one of the bridges over the Barnā (Duncan's bridge), forty-eight statues and other sculptured stones were removed from Sārnāth and thrown into the river, to serve as a breakwater to the piers; and that in the erection of the second bridge, the iron one, from fifty to sixty cart-loads of stones from the Sārnāth buildings were employed".

General Cunningham's excavations were followed by those of Major Markham Kittoe, "Archæological Engineer" to the Government in 1851-52, who was then employed in designing and building the Queen's College at Benares. He excavated numerous *stūpas* "four and five deep built one over the other", around the Dhamekh Stūpa, and the greater part of a quadrangular structure to the west of the latter *stūpa* which he identified as a hospital because he found in it a number of stone mortars and pestles. The recent excavations have shown that it was, in reality, a monastery of the usual type. Major Kittoe also commenced the clearance of another monastery, which has since then been designated as Kittoe's monastery. His excavations were continued first by Mr. E. Thomas, C.S., a Judge and coin collector, and afterwards by Mr. Fitz Edward Hall, Professor at the Queen's College. Some digging was also carried out by Mr. C. Horn, C.S., in 1865; and Mr. A. Rivett Carnac, C.S., discovered a Buddha image in 1877. We do not hear of any further excavations on this site until the year 1905, though excavations for materials by contractors and villagers must have continued even during this interval.

The excavations described above extended over a hundred years or more and it might well have been thought that the site had yielded up all its antiquarian treasures especially because General Cunningham had already recorded his opinion that no further excavations on this site were advisable. Recent explorations have, however, shown how untenable General Cunningham's conclusion was, for it is now evident that he had totally failed to penetrate the lower and earlier strata where lay buried antiquities of greater value and interest. These new excavations were first conducted, with the sanction and advice of the Archæological Department, by Mr. F. O. Oertel in the cold weather of 1904-05. Mr. Oertel unearthed the Main Shrine, the Asoka Column with its magnificent capital and a galaxy of *stūpas* all round it, as well as a very large number of sculptures and inscriptions.

The excavations remained in abeyance in the year 1905-06 but in 1907 they were resumed under the personal supervision of Sir John Marshall, with the assistance of Dr. Sten Konow, then Government Epigraphist for India, Mr. Nicholls and the writer of this handbook. These operations, which were carried on for two consecutive seasons, embraced the whole of the northern portion of the acquired area, and the areas on all the four sides of the Main Shrine and supplied, for the first time, the real key to the ancient topography of the site. It was then found that the Main Shrine with the pillar and the *stūpa* of Asoka constituted the nucleus around which the numerous other structures which we now see at Sārnāth were erected as time rolled by. The most important of the buildings brought to light by the Director General were three monasteries of the late Kushāna period and a fourth and extensive building which was constructed upon the ruins of all these three monasteries in the late mediæval period. All these buildings must originally have been very imposing edifices which religious zeal of the highest order could alone have called into being. There was no work done at Sārnāth again for five or six years, but in 1914-15, Mr. Hargreaves carried out some very successful excavations in the areas to the east, north and west of the Main Shrine. In the last mentioned area he laid bare the remains of an early apsidal temple and a large mass of fragmentary sculptures of the Sunga period (see p. 4 above). An equally remarkable result of his excavations was the discovery of three standing images of the Buddha, the inscriptions engraved on which have led to a considerable modification of the accepted scheme of the Gupta genealogy.*

The operations conducted by myself during the years 1917-22 included, on the one hand, the general clearance and improvement of the acquired area and the conservation of the buildings laid bare in the previous explorations and, on the other hand, excavations in different

* *Vide* "The dates of Skandagupta and his successors" by Mr. Panna Lal, I.C.S., in the "Hindustan Review" for January, 1918.

parts of the site. The most important undertakings of the latter description were the examination of the unexplored portions of the areas between the Dhamekh Stūpa and the Main Shrine and the site of Monastery II. The former was at one time believed to be an ancient tank and was consequently filled up with excavated earth in 1904-05. The excavations now carried out have brought back to view a large open courtyard, measuring 271′×112′ which must have been added to the Main Shrine about the 8th or 9th century A. D. The original drain which carried off water from this court and the Main Shrine has also been found and completely exhumed for the whole of its length. The object of the examination of the area occupied by Monastery II was to ascertain the real character of an interesting structure which was partially excavated in 1907-08. It has now been completely laid bare and turns out to be a shrine with a long covered underground passage, such as would be most suitable for the monks' retirement into solitude for the performance of spiritual practices.

The Benares School of Sculpture.

The various schools of sculptural art practised in ancient times in Northern and Central India and their relationship to one another have been discussed in detail by Sir John Marshall and Dr. Vogel in the Annual Reports of the Archæological Survey of India. The existence of an independent style at Benares and the neighbouring districts has been recognised ever since the commencement of systematic exploration at Sārnāth about 28 years ago. Here it will be sufficient to insert a brief summary of the main conclusions about the origin and general characteristics of the sculptures discovered at Sārnāth and the Gupta art in general.

The finest and oldest sculptures so far unearthed at Sārnāth are the bell-shaped Capital of the Asoka pillar in Perso-Hellenistic style and the monolithic railing which originally surmounted the Dharmarājikā Stūpa. These monuments with others of the same period constitute a class by themselves. Their main peculiarity is their dependence on Persian originals, specimens of which are still extant in that country, and their lustrous polish which is mainly responsible for their preservation. The art of giving such a high polish to stone was also learnt by Indian artists from their contemporaries of Persia, but it went out of use in India about the 1st Century B. C. and has not as yet been noticed in any later monuments. But while the technique of execution of the Sārnāth Capital is in every sense foreign, it is evident that in accordance with the prevailing Indian custom, the carving was done under the guidance of a learned Buddhist monk conversant with the scripture. The placing of the wheel symbolizing the Buddhist Wheel of Righteousness at the summit of the pillar was a happy idea which must be credited to the ingenuity of the same monk. It was no doubt he, too, who suggested the utilization of the circular abacus for the representation of an appropriate motive from the Buddhist texts. The interpretation of the four animals figured in bold relief on this member has been a matter of conjecture. There is, however, very good reason to believe that the circular drum with the four animals is intended to illustrate the Anotatta, one of the eight great lakes of the Buddhist system of cosmogony (see page 40).

To the late Maurya or Sunga period belong, besides the railing posts mentioned above, a large number of the sculptures and architectural stones which came to light in the area to the west of the Asoka Pillar and are characterised by the same kind of polish as the Asoka monuments mentioned above.

On the other hand, the eleven posts (*Da* 1 to 11), which belonged to a railing of the Āndhra period, appertain to the indigenous school as we find exhibited in the monuments of Bharhut, Bodh Gayā and Sānchī. The posts are adorned with a variety of symbols, most interesting of which are *stūpas* surrounded with railings, a *chaitya* hall, a leaf hut, and the trident representing the three jewels, *viz.*, the Buddha, the good law and the Buddhist Church.

The most glorious period of the Benares School was the Gupta epoch and corresponded approximately to the period 350 to 650 A. D. It is aptly called the Golden Age of the Indian History. Northern India had suffered for more than three centuries under the alien yoke of the Kushānas, Parthians and the Sakas. The accession of this family of indigenous kings ushered in a new era of all-round progress and advancement such as had not been experienced since the collapse of the great Maurya Empire. The results of this new activity are summarised in the following remarks of Sir John Marshall. Says he, " thus, the Gupta age marked a re-awakening—a true ' Renaissance ' of the Indian intellect; and the new intellectualism was reflected in architecture and the formative arts as much as in other spheres of knowledge and thought. Indeed, it is precisely in their intellectual qualities—in their logical thought and logical beauty—that the architecture and sculpture of the Gupta age stand pre-eminent in the history of Indian art, and that they remind us in many respects of the creations of Greece 800 years earlier or of Italy a thousand years later ". The Gupta kings were all followers of the Brahmanical Hindu faith and naturally their best efforts were directed towards the regeneration of the early Brahmanical institutions, such as the Asvamedha sacrifice,* the revival of the Sanskrit language and literature and the endowment of Brahmanical religious establishments. Some of the most noteworthy foundations of this period are the beautiful

* A well preserved horse statue in the Provincial Museum at Lucknow with the name of the Gupta king, Samudragupta, engraved on its neck is believed to be a memorial of a horse sacrifice performed by that Emperor.

brick temples at Bhitargaon and other places in the Cawnpore District, the Vaishnava pillar and colossal statue of the Boar incarnation at Eran, the Garuda standard erected by Skandagupta at Kahaon, in the Gorakhpur District, the beautiful Gupta temple at Deogarh and last though not the least the celebrated iron pillar at old Delhi.

The Gupta kings were, however, no narrow-minded sectarians. Samudragupta who took much delight in the society of learned men, showed favour to Vasubandhu, the famous Buddhist author, and we possess Fa-Hian's reliable testimony to show that during the Gupta rule the Buddhists enjoyed perfect freedom of worship and full liberty to endow their sacred places. The sculptures excavated at Sārnāth include at least three Buddha images which in the inscriptions engraved on them are described as having been installed in the years 154 (A. D. 473) and 157 (A. D. 476) of the Gupta era in the reigns of Kumāragupta and Budhagupta respectively. Under the later Gupta kings of Valabhi, Buddhism continued to flourish as it had done under the Imperial Guptas and in the 6th or 7th century their capital was the residence of renowned Buddhist teachers and an important seat of Buddhist learning. In the 7th century Buddhism received further impetus from the benevolent government of Harshavardhana, who ruled over Northern India from 606 to 647 A. D. Though himself a worshipper of Siva and the Sun, he was a zealous patron of Buddhism and endeavoured to do for this doctrine what Asoka had done for it more than 800 years before him. He received the Chinese pilgrim Hiuen Tsang in two crowded assemblies held at Kanauj and Prayāga (modern Allahabad) and showed honours of the highest order to the image of the Buddha.

The sculptures preserved in the Sārnāth Museum which have all been unearthed at Sārnāth itself represent the historical Buddha, before and after his enlightenment, several other Bodhisattvas and gods and goddesses of the later or Mahāyāna School of Buddhism propounded by Nāgārjuna and other teachers in the 1st or 2nd century A. D. These images explain their own origin and growth. The early Indian sculptures of the Maurya, Sunga and early Andhra periods referred to above include no images of the Buddha because he had not yet become deified and consequently no images of him were made. In these circumstances the discovery of a colossal stone statue (*Ba* 1) of the Kushāna period in the area between the Main Shrine and the Dharmarājikā Stūpa proved exceedingly useful as it turns out to be at once the starting point and the prototype on which the Buddhist images of Sārnāth are based. The red sandstone in which it is fashioned, the schematic treatment of the robes and the large halo with a plain border point to its having been a product of the sculptors of Mathurā while the inscriptions engraved on it supply the further information that it was carved under the supervision of a monk of Mathurā and brought over and installed in the 3rd year of the reign of Kānishka, in Benares, *i.e.*, at Sārnāth on the promenade of the Blessed One.

The arrival of this statue at Sārnāth must have been so welcome that local artists at once set to work and the Sārnāth Museum contains two statues (*Ba* 2 and 3) which are almost exact copies of the one from Mathurā.

The Sārnāth types of Buddha and Bodhisattva images which followed are rightly regarded as the finest creations of the Gupta period. It was no wonder, therefore, that this new art so rapidly spread not only to the rest of India, but also to the neighbouring countries of Siam, Kambodia and Ceylon.

The main characteristics of the Mathurā images of the Kushāna period have been indicated above. The Sārnāth images differ in several essential points; the most remarkable being the replacement of the flat and Mongolian type of the former school by a figure of much higher beauty distinguished by round and supple limbs, and the lifelike delineation of hands, fingers, etc. An equally striking feature of the Sārnāth images is the total disappearance of the conventional folds of drapery which here yield place to close-fitting and transparent robes merely distinguished by their edges round the neck, across the chest and on the lower legs. The cult of the Bodhisattva received special attention at Sārnāth, and we have here images of almost all the deities of this class that were recognised and honoured by the Mahāyānists of this period. Nor are we left in doubt, as we so often are in Gandhāra and Mathurā, about the identity of their statues. In accordance with his character of a friar, the Buddha is invariably dressed in the three garments (Sanskrit *trichīvara*), prescribed for monks. The Bodhisattvas, being heirs apparent to Buddhahood, have secular attire and wear diadems and ornaments.

There is, however, a decided falling off in the delineation of the events of the earthly life and the previous existences (Sanskrit *Jātaka*) of the Buddha. The Gandhāra sculptures are literally a "Buddha Story in Stone" and there is no episode of any consequence, whether real or legendary, which is not depicted. Such representations are less varied and numerous at Mathurā. At Sārnāth they are restricted to the eight main events (see page 45 *infra*). The only Jātaka scene so far identified with certainty at Sārnāth is the Kshāntivādi-Jātaka carved on the large lintel (No. *Dd* 1).

The Benares artists continued their craft at Sārnāth until the end of the 12th century when it was completely destroyed by the Muhammadan invaders. The sculptures of the mediæval period (Circa 650—1200) in the Sārnāth Museum will be easily distinguished by their inferior technique and sometimes uncanonical delineation. There are, however, some valuable exceptions.

THE MONUMENTS.

Chaukhandi.

This is the name of a large ruined structure which the visitor to Sārnāth passes to the left of the road half a mile before reaching the main site. The monument consists of a lofty mound of brickwork locally known as Chaukhandi, or the "square edifice" surmounted with an octagonal tower making a total height of 84 feet from the level of the ground. The octagonal tower is much later than the ruined structure underneath it, for, according to a Persian inscription engraved on a stone slab over its northern doorway, it was erected by the Mughal Emperor Akbar, in the Hijrī year 996, corresponding to 1588 A. D., to commemorate a visit to this spot by his father Humāyūn. An ascent to the top of the tower affords an extensive and pleasing view of the country around, the most interesting landmarks being the Dhamekh Stūpa of Sārnāth to the north, and the slender minarets of the mosque of Aurangzeb in the Hindu city of Benares to the south. It is interesting to observe that the two minarets of the mosque appear as one, the front one hiding the other, and thus showing that the mound is situated nearly due north of that mosque.

Mr. Oertel exposed the lower parts of the *stūpa** in 1904-05. We find that it stood on a basement consisting of three square terraces each about twelve feet broad and the same in height. The *stūpa* itself has disappeared, but a portion of its plinth, which remains above the highest platform, is octagonal in plan with star-like points at the angles. Another fact revealed by the excavations is that, whereas the core of the structure is composed of solid brickwork laid in clay mortar, the terraces are supported on rows of hollow cells. The outer walls of the terraces were adorned with panels separated by brick pilasters. Among the sculptures that came to light in the excavation of this structure were two sculptured slabs showing leogryphs ridden by human warriors,† which presumably adorned the flank walls of the stair which led up to the top of the basement of the *stūpa*.

---

* A *stūpa* is a solid tower, which was built either to enshrine the corporeal remains of a saint or other great personage, or as a memorial of some remarkable event. Edifices of this kind were erected by the Jainas as well as by the Buddhists. According to the Buddhist texts the corporeal remains of Buddhas or universal kings only were considered fit to be enshrined in *stūpas*. In later times, however, even ordinary Buddhist monks and teachers received this distinction. The earliest form of the *stūpa* was hemispheric like the inverted bowl of a Buddhist monk. According to a legend quoted by Hiuen Tsang (Beal, *Buddhist Records of the Western World*, Vol. I, page 47) this design was prescribed by the Buddha himself. Two merchants, named Tapassu and Bhalluka, had received from the Master for worship some of his hair and nail cuttings and asked of him the right way of venerating the relics. "Tathāgata forthwith spreading out his *Sanghāti* on the ground as a square napkin, next laid down his *Uttarāsanga* and then his *Sankakshikā*; again over these he placed as a cover his begging pot, on which he erected his mendicant's staff. Thus he placed them in order, making thereby (the figure of) a *stūpa*." This was the first *stūpa* of the Buddhist religion and is said to be identical with the far-famed Shwedagun at Rangoon.

† These are now preserved in the Sārnāth Museum and are numbered Cb 1 and 2.

In 1835 A. D., General Cunningham sank a well into the structure from the floor of the octagonal tower of Akbar down to the virgin soil. As he did not find any relics in it, he concluded that it must be a memorial *stūpa* and identified it as the one raised on the spot where Gautama Buddha, when coming from Gayā to Sārnāth, first met the five recluses, Kaundinya and the rest, to whom a reference has been made above. This identification appears to be most plausible, as the position of the Chaukhandi Stūpa agrees almost precisely with the bearing and distance of the said *stūpa* from the Deer-Park, and there is no other *stūpa* in this direction which would answer to the description recorded by the Chinese pilgrim. The *stūpa* noticed by Hiuen Tsang on this spot is stated to have been 300 feet in height and Mr. Oertel's estimate of 200 feet for the existing structure when complete is a near approximation.

The brick platform with a flag, by the side of the big mound, is modern. Here the villagers sacrifice goats for the propitiation of evil spirits.

The Deer-Park.

Half a mile to the north on the road we come to the Deer-Park itself. The new stone building we notice on our right hand side is the Archæological Museum in which have been arranged all the well-preserved portable antiquities discovered on this site. It is, however, advisable to go over the ancient buildings first. For the convenience of the visitor, a red line has been shown in the accompanying plan to indicate the route which he is recommended to follow when going over the remains of the Deer-Park.

The Southern Area.

It has been customary hitherto to divide the portion of the Deer-Park that has so far been explored into two distinct areas, namely, the Stūpa Area on the South and the Monastery Area on the North. In view of the new experience gained, that division no longer appears to hold good. In point of fact, the temples and *stūpas* occupy the central portion of the site, the areas round about them being occupied by monasteries.

Monastery VI.

(Kittoe's Monastery.)

Immediately on entering the site we notice on our right the remains of a Buddhist Monastery (No. VI) occupying a much lower level than the road. This monument has hitherto been designated as Kittoe's Monastery, because, as stated above, it was mainly exposed by his excavations in the year 1851-52. Major Kittoe died before publishing an account of his operations at this monastery, but General Cunningham has left us in his Archæological Survey Reports, Volume

I, a fairly complete account of the monument, derived from letters received by him from the explorer himself. This information is to the effect that the monastery originally measured 107 feet along each side externally and, like most Buddhist convents known to us, consisted of an open courtyard surrounded by passages supported on pillars to give access to ranges of cells on all four sides. We further learn that the rooms in the monastery numbered twenty-eight, which were as usual small cubicles, each one just big enough to accommodate a single monk or nun and furnished with a separate door. The central room of the north row which was larger than the others was identified by General Cunningham as the sanctuary of the monastery, for though no images had been found in it, the stone pedestals on which they stood were still extant. He believed the monastery to have been entered from the south and held that a square elaborately carved block of stone laid bare in the centre room on this side must have served as "the seat of the teacher for the daily reading and expounding of the Buddhist scriptures".

Since General Cunningham's time, the greater part of this monastery had perished and there was so little left on the surface that the very plan had become obscure and scarcely recognisable as that of a *saṅghārāma*. A little excavation was clearly necessary and several new facts emerge from it. In the first place it becomes evident that the large room in the centre of the northern range which General Cunningham believed to be the chapel of the monastery is, in reality, the entrance chamber which gave access to the interior of the building. The three small rooms which project from the outer wall, and which General Cunningham entirely overlooked, are the portico and guard-rooms, similar to those usually met with in other monasteries of this and later periods. The large blocks of stone which were then mistaken for pedestals of images really formed the threshold of the entrance hall, the mortices which remain in them having been meant to receive the tenons of the jambs of the doorway. The chapel of the monastery must, therefore, have been situated in the southern row of apartments just opposite the entrance and could have been no other than the centre room on that side. In the second place we learn that this monastery contained at least one more court on the east side which still lies buried under the ground adjoining the modern shed for Brahmanical sculptures. Lastly, it is observed that whereas the monastery excavated by Major Kittoe was presumably constructed in the mediæval period, underneath it lie the foundations of an earlier one whose floor level was about two feet lower than that of the later structure. This fact was brought to light by an examination of the two cells in the south-west corner of the building which had remained unexplored in the previous excavations. These cells showed two distinct floors laid one over the other and as the upper floor yielded a terra-cotta sealing with the Buddhist creed in characters of about the ninth century A. D., this must be the approximate date of the later monastery. On the lower floor were found about a dozen sealings belonging to the Gandha-kuṭi of the Holy One and assignable on palæographical grounds to the sixth or seventh century A. D. The earlier monastery is, however, much older than these sealings, as the bricks of which it is composed are of a large size equal to 17½″×11″×2½″, which is generally met with in the Kushāna or even earlier monuments.

The well in the middle of the court-yard is coeval with the foundation of the original monastery. The water of this well is sweet and is eagerly drunk by Buddhist visitors to the site.

From the evidence of the thickness of its walls, General Cunningham concluded that this monastery must have had three or four storeys and been one of the thirty monasteries seen by the Chinese pilgrim Hiuen Tsang in the seventh century A. D.

Major Kittoe's excavations gave ample proof of the fact that the monastery had been destroyed by a great fire applied by the hand of a hostile invader. The conflagration was " so sudden and rapid as to force the monks to abandon their very food " for the explorer found " the remains of ready made wheaten cakes, in a small recess ". I myself found in the two cells referred to above, several earthen pots containing remnants of cooked rice.

MONASTERY NO. VII.

The structure immediately to the west of the monastery just described, which was brought to light in the year 1918, is a small building of the same type constructed on the usual plan with a paved courtyard, 30 feet square, in the centre and a well preserved brick well near the north-east corner. All the cells of the monastery, which surrounded the central courtyard on all sides have disappeared but portions of the front walls of the cells, and the paved verandah are partly preserved. The bases of a few of the stone columns which supported the roof of the passage have also survived in position. The high level of the structure, the smallness of its dimensions and the material consisting of brickbats empolyed in its construction all point to its being one of the latest foundations on the site. This view is supported by the evidence of late mediæval inscriptions found in the clearance of the well referred to. One of these inscribed objects is a terra-cotta seal matrix (1¼″ in diameter) which contains in reversed characters the name of a certain Srī-Sishyada, who might have endowed this hospice for the residence of monks. We might also mention a thin sheet of copper, with edges turned down in the form of a packet. It bears the well known Buddhist formula, and was probably an amulet of some sort.

The shattered condition of the bases of the verandah columns as also of the brick paving in the interior shows that this building probably fell a prey to the same conflagration as destroyed its larger neighbour (Monastery VI), like which it stands on the ruins of an earlier structure.

THE DHARMARĀJIKĀ STUPA.

A little further on in the plan, a red line starts from the road towards the north-west. This is the path we shall take in going over the various buildings described below. And the first object which arrests the eye on the left is the ruin of the large brick *stūpa* which was demolished by Jagat Singh in 1794 A. D., and has hitherto been inappropriately named after him to distinguish it from other *stūpas* existing at Sārnāth. In its relic-chamber, Jagat Singh found a green arble casket which was enclosed in a bigger stone. The casket contained a few bones, some decayed pearls, etc., which were committed to the Ganges. The outer stone is now in the Indian Museum, Calcutta, but the casket has disappeared. In the same structure, though evidently at a higher level, Jagat Singh found an inscribed Buddha image the base of which is now preserved in the Archæological Museum at Sārnāth (Bc 1). The inscription engraved on the sculpture records that in the year Samvat 1083 (1026 A. D.) in the reign of Mahīpāla of Gauda (Bengal), two brothers named Sthirapāla and Vasantapāla restored a *stūpa* of Asoka and the entire establishment of the Deer-Park and also repaired a stone temple " of the eight great places"*. The Asoka *stūpa* referred to in this epigraph is probably the Jagat Singh *stūpa* itself whose name has in the present edition of the Guide been altered to Dharmarājikā *stūpa*†. The temple of the eight great places has not yet been identified.

The depredations of Jagat Singh had reduced the structure to a mere shell, the superstructure and the core having been totally removed. In spite of this, the excavations carried out in 1907-08 around the base of this *stūpa* have ascertained for us a fairly complete history of the monument. It is now found that the outer shell of the *stūpa* consists of concentric rings of brickwork, and this is all that is left of the several rebuildings undergone by the monument at different periods. The original structure, which, as stated above, must have been erected by Asoka at the same time as his inscribed pillar, is only forty-nine feet in diameter while the latest casing has a diameter of about 110 feet. The bricks of which the original structure is composed are of large dimensions like

---

* Probably the eight great places connected with the Buddha's life are meant. It is also possible that these eight great places are those where the Buddha's relics were deposited, namely, Rājagriha, Vaisālī, Kapilavastu, Allakappa, Rāmagrāma, Vethadīpa, Pāvā and Kusinagara, *cf.* p. 3 above.

† The Chinese pilgrim Hiuen Tsang mentions two Asoka *stūpas* near Benares, one of which marked the spot where Gautama Buddha began " to turn the Wheel of the Law ". These must be identical with the *stūpa* destroyed by Jagat Singh and the early brick *stūpa* on which the Dhamekh *stūpa* now stands.

those of other Asokan buildings and are of three different sizes. Most of the bricks are slightly wedge-shaped, the smaller end being laid nearer the centre of the *stūpa*, but no effort seems to have been made to bond the courses together. As is usual in the *stūpas* of this period, the Dharmarājikā *stūpa* at Sārnāth was nearly hemispheric in form though it is difficult to say whether the same form was maintained in the later enlargements. One thing, however, seems certain and it is that the original Asoka *stūpa** was like the *stūpas* recently restored at Sānchī, crowned with an umbrella and a stone railing. The umbrella has not yet been found†, but the railing may be seen lying in the southern chapel of the Main Shrine. It must have fallen down from the summit of the Dharamarājikā *stūpa* at an early date, but when precisely this took place will perhaps never be ascertained.

The first rebuilding of the *stūpa* appears to have taken place in the early centuries of the Christian era, and the second about the 5th or 6th century A. D. The circular processional path (Sanskrit *pradakshina*), portions of which were exposed in 1907-08, must have been added at the latter rebuilding. This passage is 15 to 16 feet wide. The encircling wall, which is 4′ 5″ high, was pierced with doorways at each of the cardinal points, just as are the railings round the *stūpas* of Bhārhut and Sānchī. The next addition is referable to about the 7th century A. D., and included the filling up of the processional path. Access was then gained to the *stūpa* by four flights of steps, cut out of single blocks of stone, all of which have been laid bare. A short inscription on the topmost step of the stair on the south side dates from the 2nd or 3rd century A. D., but the steps themselves are probably earlier than that date. The latest or eighth rebuilding took place about the 11th century A. D., and must have been coeval with the erection of the Dharmachakra-Jinavihāra.

The numerous smaller structures exposed all round the Dharmarājikā Stūpa are mostly votive or memorial structures raised by pilgrims as tokens of their visits in the mediæval period. One of these, situated to the west of the big *stūpa*, had an inscribed Buddha statuette in a niche. The image dates from about the 5th century A. D., and must have been rescued from an earlier building. It will be seen that a few *stūpas* to the north of the Dharmarājikā have, like it, been rebuilt several times.

A short distance to the north of the Dharmarājikā Stūpa, halfway between it and the Main Shrine, was found the colossal red sand-

* This fact is of considerable interest, for, if this *stūpa*, as seems probable, was in reality erected by Asoka, the bones that were found in the green marble casket referred to in the text may have been a portion of Gautama Buddha's own corporeal remains.

† A small piece of the top of an umbrella (A 2 in the Museum Catalogue) in typical Maurya style which was found in 1906-07 may have formed part of the umbrella which originally surmounted the Dharmarājikā *stūpa*.

stone statue of Buddha with its umbrella [B (*a*) 1 in the Museum], which was carved at Mathurā and erected at Sārnāth in the 1st century A. D.

The Main Shrine.

The next building which rises before us as we proceed northward is a conspicuous structure situated some twenty yards north of the Dharmarājikā Stūpa and distinguished in the Plan of Excavations as the Main Shrine. This building has hitherto been assigned to about the eleventh century A. D., but its style of construction and material make it several centuries earlier. The temple consisted originally of a single hall 45′ 6″ square internally, the walls being 10′ thick. From the north, west and south sides project rectangular chapels which are only entered from the outside. There was no chapel on the east side, its place being taken, of necessity, by a portico in front of the entrance. The walls of this building are now nowhere standing to a greater height than 18 feet. The inside walls appear to have been quite plain, but externally the Main Shrine was decorated with a variety of mouldings consisting of full and half torus patterns, circular niches containing pilasters with vase-shaped bases and bracket capitals and other motifs, all reminiscent of good Gupta work. As far as the walls exist, these mouldings are continued on all sides of the building without interruption. There is similar homogeneity noticed everywhere in the material of which the building is composed, for with the exception of the door-frames and some later underpinning in the bases of the walls, the entire construction, including the ponderous core is in whole bricks ranging in size from $14\frac{1}{2}'' \times 8\frac{1}{2}'' \times 2\frac{1}{4}''$ to $15\frac{1}{2}'' \times 9\frac{1}{2}'' \times 2\frac{1}{8}''$, and laid in mud mortar. The enormous thickness of the walls suggests a lofty superstructure, which might have been a high pyramidal spire like that of the principal temple at Bodh Gayā.

At a later date, which it is difficult to determine with certainty, the roof of the temple began to show signs of weakness and the addition of the massive wall eleven feet in thickness which now runs round three sides of the interior would appear to have been provided to prevent its collapse. The cella was thus reduced to a square chamber of 23′ 6″ along each side. It was presumably at this time that the large rectangular platform at the back of the shrine was constructed to support the image that was worshipped in it. This image was probably destroyed centuries ago, for like many other ancient statues rescued by pious repairers from earlier strata, it must have been visible at the time of the invasion of the Deer-Park in the 12th century and broken to pieces.

The chapels on the north and west sides have lost their images though the brick platforms on which they rested are intact. In the chapel on the south side was found a headless standing statue of Buddha in the posture of granting security and in Gupta style. The images that originally existed in the other two chapels would appear to have been similar to this image. It was wise of Mr. Oertel to have cut through the floor of this chapel, as it disclosed an important relic of the Asoka period, namely, a square monolithic railing of the usual Maurya type which encloses within it a comparatively unimportant brick *stūpa*. The railing is cut out of a single block of sandstone which must have been quarried at Chunar in the Mirzapur District and exhibits the same skilful workmanship and high polish as characterise other art products of the time of Asoka. The railing was square in plan, 8′ 4″ along each side and 4′ 9″ in height, with four square uprights and three lozenge-shaped cross-bars on each side.

So far, two ancient inscriptions have been noticed on this balustrade, one on the front of the base on the east side and the other on the south side. Both the epigraphs indicate that the railing was in the possession of the teachers of the Sarvāstivādi sect in the 3rd or 4th century A. D. to which date these inscriptions should be assigned on palæographical grounds. A careful examination of the inscription on the east side will, however, reveal the fact that the last word of this record is a remnant of an earlier inscription which was written in a script of the first or second century B. C., and in the Prākrit or vernacular dialect of that period. The rest of the epigraph obviously contained the name of some other sect of the Buddhists. It was rubbed off in the 3rd or 4th century A. D. by the teachers of the Sarvāstivādi sect who substituted their own name in place of that of the older sect. This alteration was evidently made by the later sect to assert their own superiority at Sārnāth. It was for the same reason too, that the inscription as altered was re-engraved on the south side of the railing in the Sanskrit language. The small brick *stūpa* inside the railing was opened up in 1906-07, but yielded no relics of any kind.

In its present condition, the Asoka railing is incomplete, nearly half of the monument having been broken off and lost. It is evident that it does not occupy its actual position and the purpose for which it was originally carved was a matter of conjecture for several years. Two suggestions were considered most plausible, namely, that either this balustrade was erected to protect some sacred object, possibly marking the very spot where the Buddha was supposed to have sat while " turning the Wheel of the Law " or that it surrounded the base of the Asoka pillar. Both these views are found to be erroneous. For it is now evident, as stated above (p. 18), that this railing originally surrounded the umbrella or *hti* on the top of the Dharmarājikā *stūpa*. Perhaps it was thrown down by a violent earthquake.

The above remarks will show that the original erection of the Main Shrine must have taken place about the Gupta period, but who built it we do not yet know. The original floor level inside the building would appear to have been approximately the same as that of the base of the Asoka railing in the southern chapel. In the latter chamber the Asoka balustrade presumably remained visible, through the centuries, being approached by a later flight of steps, when the level around the Main Shrine had arisen. The existing entrances of the three chapels belong to two different periods. The earlier door-frames which are painted red and carved with bands of scroll work appear to date from about the 7th century A. D. The later ones are quite plain. It was no doubt at this late period that the lower portions of the walls on the outside were repaired in a very careless fashion with stones obtained from Gupta and later structures. The two or three inscribed blocks at the outer south-west corner of the building bearing the name *Suhilah* in Nāgarī characters of the late mediæval period and inserted in the face of the wall, the wrong way up, manifestly formed part of these repairs. It is these stones which have been, in the main, responsible for the misunderstanding that has prevailed since the excavation of this monument, about the actual date of its construction. For it has been argued that as these stones, about the lateness of which there can be no doubt, form part of its construction, the Main Shrine must have been erected at a still later date. It is, however, now obvious that these stones were inserted during some very late repairs and had nothing to do with the original design.

The above remarks coupled with the central position of the Main Shrine and its close proximity to the Asokan monuments appear conclusively to prove its identity with the temple which according to Hiuen Tsang marked the spot where the Buddha had sat down to deliver his first sermon.

Around the Main Shrine, the excavations laid bare a thick concrete floor which extended some forty feet in every direction, and must have been renewed or added to several times. Beyond this pavement on the east side there was a broad paved approach which at the time of the previous edition of this handbook had been exposed for a length of over 150 feet. The recent excavations carried out by the writer have revealed the fact that the broad approach referred to was only a part of an extensive open court (Sanskrit *angana*), added to the Main Shrine sometime in the mediæval period. The approach yielded many valuable sculptures to the spade of Sir John Marshall in 1906-07 and 1907-08 while two or three sculptures with Gupta inscriptions of the reigns of Kumāragupta and Budhagupta of the Imperial Gupta dynasty were found on it in 1914-15. Reference has been made to some of these objects in the Introduction while a few others will be found described later on in the chapter dealing with the Museum.

The open court of the Main Shrine presumably measured 271 feet in length from east to west, while the width in the eastern portion averages 112 feet. It was enclosed in a brick wall on the north, south and east sides, the greater part of which has fallen down. The interior of the court was approached by a double staircase in the middle of the east wall, which is built up with stone slabs of different periods. One or two of them bear Gupta carvings.

The monuments brought to light inside the court are all *stūpas* of various sizes with the exception of two chapels, one of which stands in the south-east corner while the other is numbered 137 in the accompanying plan. The earliest of these structures go back to the Gupta period, and include a fascinating *stūpa*, No. 136, built entirely in brick whose plinth (8′ 6″ square) alone has survived. Each face of the plinth contained an elaborately designed niche which must originally have contained a Buddhist image. The rest of the surface is adorned with panels enclosed in bracket pilasters and containing beautifully carved lotus rosettes, elaborate lions' heads and other decorative devices such as were commonly employed in the stone architecture of the Gupta period. The interior of this structure has not yet been examined and we are unable to say whether it contains any relics. All round this *stūpa* plinth is a well preserved concrete floor about 1¼ feet below the level of the floor with which the interior of this enclosure is paved. This is interesting as showing how small was the accumulation of débris on this area and as furnishing a convenient standard for judging the relative ages of the structures being dealt with.

A little later in date than No. 136 is a shrine situated close to it. It measures 37′×27′ 10″ externally and at the time of excavation contained two Buddha images lying face downwards. All the other structures brought to light in this compound belong to the mediæval period. They were constructed for the most part in fulfilment of vows. Among these, six or seven *stūpas* arranged in a line along the southern portion of the east wall of the court are most prominent and unlike the other *stūpas* on this site, are composed of stone. They are all relic *stūpas* or Dagobas (Sanskrit *Dhātugarbha*) as they contain the remains of some of the deceased Buddhist saints who lived and died at Sārnāth.

The chapel in the south-east corner of the courtyard dates from the same period as the Dharmachakra-Jinavihāra. This is evident from the flat and stencil-like carvings which characterise the masonry in both these monuments. The shrine must have been built in the usual Northern Indian style with a tapering spire and a small square cella preceded by a smaller portico. That the temple was dedicated to Vārāhī* or Mārichi, the goddess of the dawn, is shown by the existence of the pedestal of the cult image in its original position against the back wall of the shrine. It is carved with figures of the said goddess in seated and standing postures,

* The small hamlet named Baraipur situated about two furlongs to the north-east of the Dhamekh Stūpa presumably derived its name from this very temple.

while the male and female figures appearing at both ends of the pedestal may be identified as the donor and his wife. The image itself must have been removed or destroyed before the shrine was unearthed in 1918-19. At a later date this shrine, like one or two others on this site, was appropriated for Brahmanical worship, for in its south-east corner was lying a well preserved seated image (ht. 2′ 6″, width 1′ 3″) representing one of the aspects of Bhairava, as also a small pedestal containing a group of five Siva-*lingas*.

An important feature of this courtyard is a well built drain 1′ 8″ to 2′ 7″ in width and 3 feet deep which carried away rain water from the whole of this area and which was exposed during the operations of 1921-22. It is composed of brickbats and covered with hammer-dressed slabs with a large admixture of architectural members of sorts such as fragments of lintels, posts of railings, umbrella tops and the like. The channel starts from the north-east corner of the enclosure and after a length of 250 feet runs underneath the foundation of gateway II of the Dharmachakra-Jinavihāra. This circumstance furnishes unmistakable proof of the latter building being a good deal later than the original construction of the Main Shrine. Attention may also here be drawn to a brick-lined reservoir or *kunda* with sloping sides about five feet deep and seven feet square at the top, which came to light outside the court adjoining the flight of steps. This tank, like the one laid bare by Dr. Vogel in Monastery L. M. at Kasiá, must have been kept filled up with water with which monks and nuns could purify their hands and feet before entering the sacred precinct, more especially on occasions of the *Uposatha* ceremony on the New Moon (Amāvāsyā) and Full Moon (Pūrnimā) *tithis*, when they assembled for their confession of sins (Sanskrit *vinayadharma*)..

Only one other structure on the east side of the Main Shrine deserves special mention. This is the large rectangular court marked 36 in the Plan of Excavations and situated immediately in front of the entrance to the Main Shrine, its floor level being a few feet below the level of the temple. It was probably a lecture hall. At the time of excavation, it was hidden under the terraced floor surrounding the Main Shrine. The thinness of its walls shows that the structure had either no roof at all or only a light wooden one supported on columns of the same material. Against its back wall we notice a solid brick platform which would appear to have been reserved for the use of the teacher or chairman of the congregation. The south, west and north walls were protected on the outside with a railing of the usual type, a small portion of which has come down on the north wall. A stone (Da 39) which belonged to the coping of this balustrade bears an inscription of about the 2nd century B. C., though the building to which it is now attached must be somewhat later in date.

The numerous structures unearthed on the south, west and north sides of the Main Shrine are, like those on the east side of it, mostly memorials of pilgrims' visits which are of varying sizes according to the means of the donors. One compact group of *stūpas* situated to the north-east of the Main Shrine as also another group to the south-west marked some particularly hallowed spots, for here every individual structure has been rebuilt or enlarged several times over. The largest *stūpa* in the former group is that numbered 40 in the Plan of Excavations. The whole of its superstructure had disappeared, but the plinth which was dug into revealed, a little below the top, a layer of unbaked clay tablets and still lower down a number of stone sculptures of the 4th or 5th century A. D. The clay tablets contained a figure of the Buddha as seated at the moment of his enlightenment and the Buddhist creed stamped in characters of the 8th or 9th century A. D. It is clear that these tablets and the sculptures must have been built into this structure on the occasion of a reconstruction probably in the late mediæval period.

We may also notice here another *stupa* marked 13 in the Plan of Excavations and situated to the north-west of the Main Shrine, as it was near this structure that the stone umbrella fragment bearing the Pāli inscription referred to above (p. 2) was found.

THE ASOKA PILLAR.

We may now turn to the Asoka Pillar, which was brought to light by Mr. Oertel a few yards to the west of the Main Shrine in 1904-05. The capital and some fragments of the shaft were found lying close to the western wall of the Main Shrine. The lower portion of the column, which is standing *in situ*, protruded slightly above the concrete floor which surrounds the Main Shrine. The destruction of the Asoka Pillar must, therefore, have taken place several centuries after the erection of the Main Shrine. The stump of the column, which is in position, is about 17 feet high with a diameter of about 2′ 6″ at the bottom; and judging from the broken fragments that have come to light, the whole original height of the column including the lion capital must have been about 50 feet. The column rests on a large slab of stone measuring 8′×6′×1′ 6″. Like the other Asoka pillars, the one at Sārnāth was a monolith cut out of a single block of sand-stone quarried at Chunar some 20 miles south of Benares. The shaft supported a magnificent lion capital, 7 feet high, which in its turn was crowned with a stone wheel 2′ 9″ in diameter*.

* For a representation of a complete Asoka Pillar, showing the shaft, the capital, the abacus, the lions and the crowning wheel of the Law, the reader is referred to Mr. Havell's Hand-book of Indian Art, Plate VI-B.

A similar pillar appears to be referred to in a verse of the *Kathāsaritsāgara* (Taranga 2, v. 174). This pillar was seen at Mathurā but there is nothing to show that it was really an Asoka pillar.

The capital and a few pieces of the wheel are now in the museum and will be described later on. The whole of the column has undergone a high polish so that the stone may be easily mistaken for marble. The lower 7½ feet of the shaft which is left undressed was buried in the ground from the outset, and its upper limit marks the level of the ground around the column at the time of its erection. Between this level and the concrete floor around the Main Shrine, the excavations brought to light the remains of several floors which were laid one above the other as the ground around the column gradually arose. The latest of these, which came to light three feet below the concrete floor was composed of stone slabs and measured 18′ 10″ from north to south and 16′ 9″ from east to west. 2½ feet below this floor were found four brick walls which surrounded the column and supported some sort of a platform around it. These walls were much decayed and have had to be rebuilt with old bricks obtained from the site to support the columns of a new stone pavilion which has been erected over the monument to protect from rain its polish and more especially the inscription of Asoka engraved on it. The new brick floor inside the pavilion is 2′ 9″ above the original floor around the pillar.

On the west face of the portion of the column standing *in situ* is incised the well-known edict of Asoka, the celebrated patron of Buddhism who ruled over the greater part of India from 273 to 232 B. C. The inscription consisted of eleven lines, the first two of which were destroyed when the pillar was overthrown. The rest of the record is wonderfully well preserved. The edict is composed in the vernacular of Asoka's time and purports to be a warning to the monks and nuns residing at Sārnāth against creating a schism in the Buddhist Church. In general style, the edict resembles the decrees of the Achæmenian monarchs as engraved on the rocks at Behistun. It may be translated as follows :—

" Thus saith the beloved of the gods, the Church is not to be divided. But whosoever, monk or nun, shall break up the Church, shall be made to don white garments and dwell in a place which is not a residence for the clergy. Thus must this edict be announced in the Order of Monks and in the Order of Nuns.

" Thus saith His Majesty, one such edict hath been inscribed for you in the place of assembly that there it should remain. And even such another writing ye must inscribe for the laity. The lay-people, too, should attend each fast-day in order to be inspired with faith in this edict. Also on each fast-day, without fail, every officer should attend the fast-day service to be inspired with faith in this edict and to make himself acquainted therewith.

" And as far as your district extends, ye must everywhere make known the edict according to the letter thereof. So, too, in all fortified towns and provinces, ye must cause it to be made known according to the letter thereof."

It will be observed that in this, as in other edicts of Asoka, the king is referred to merely under the epithets of *Devānam piya* and *Piyadasi lājā* meaning " the king, the beloved of the gods and the well-wisher of all ". The identity of this king with the Maurya king Asoka has now been established by an edict recently discovered near the village of Maski in the Hyderabad State, as it clearly refers to the promulgator of that commandment, as " the beloved of the gods, Asoka ".

The Asoka column also bears two other inscriptions of later dates. One of them which continues, as it were, the last line of the Asoka inscription is dated in the reign of a certain Rājā Asvaghosha in the fortieth year of the era of Kānishka. The other inscription which is assignable to the early Gupta period, that is circa 300 A. D., was recorded by the teachers of the Sammitiya sect, to which a reference has been made above.

Area to west of Asoka Pillar.

The area immediately to the west of the Asoka pillar was excavated by Mr. Hargreaves in 1914-15 down to the Maurya level. The structural remains laid bare included portions of the foundations of an apsidal temple and, above it, traces of a later monastery and other remains. The apsidal temple is built of large bricks measuring 21"×13"×4" and can hardly be posterior to the late Maurya or Sunga period. More important finds than these structural remnants were a large collection of late Maurya or Sunga fragments of elegantly carved sculptures and architectural stones, which must undoubtedly have been brought over from some other portion of the site and used as filling to level the ground. It is clear that the monuments to which these fragments belonged must have been wilfully destroyed about the late Kushāna period, but what led to this catastrophe it is impossible to say. A selection of these fragments is now exhibited in two or three show-cases in the central hall of the Archæological Museum at Sārnāth. Among them are portions of a large stone wheel resembling the one that crowned the lion capital of the Asoka pillar. This wheel may have formed part of another Asoka pillar but as the Chinese pilgrims mention only one pillar of Asoka at Sārnāth it probably belonged to a somewhat later pillar of the Sunga period. The remaining pieces include fragments of several posts and cross bars of a railing or railings, and portions of capitals of Indo-Persepolitan type which to judge from the inscriptions engraved on them were erected by the common subscriptions of certain inhabitants of Ujjayinī and Pātaliputra.

The visitor should now return to the Main Shrine and inspect a somewhat curious monument that was brought to light in 1914-15 in the area to the north of the Main Shrine. It is a circular structure with the outer diameter of 12′ 7½″, around which and separated from it by a space of 3 feet, is another concentric wall which on the east side descends to a depth of 7′ 6″. The inner structure which is composed of bricks of a very large size is seemingly an early *stūpa*, while the outer wall must have been added at a later date by a pious votary to strengthen and enlarge the structure.

Leaving the precinct of the Main Shrine, our route runs over the paved floor of a broad passage, north-east of the Main Shrine. Like the approach on the east of this building, this passage is also flanked on either side by a line of *stūpas* and other structures. In the middle of the west line was standing a large statue [B (*a*) 2 in the Museum] of Gautama Buddha of the 1st or 2nd century A. D. while near the east row was discovered the large sculptured lintel [D (*d*) 1] exhibited in the verandah of the Museum. A little distance to the north of the spot where the lintel was found, Sir John Marshall exhumed the eleven stone posts of a railing of the 1st or 2nd century B.C., which have also been transferred to the Museum.

SHRINE No. 50.

The railing referred to must originally have surrounded or surmounted a *stūpa*, perhaps the very one unearthed in the area to the north of the Main Shrine. The spot occupied by it at the time of excavation was found to be the *mandapa* of a late Gupta sanctum (No. 50 in the Plan of Excavations) which was repaired or restored in the mediaeval period. This shrine is a narrow rectangular chamber opening on east and west. The stone door-frame on the east is adorned with figures of *chauri* bearers and other carvings, while in front of the entrance and outside the north and south walls of the shrine we notice pedestals of images which were originally sheltered by stone umbrellas (Sanskrit *chhattra*). Posts of these umbrellas have survived in part. The pedestal on the south side bears an inscription in Gupta characters which states that the image was donated by a Buddhist monk named Nanala and supplies the date not only of all these images but also of the original construction of the temple. The date of the restoration of the shrine is determined approximately by the discovery of a terra-cotta tablet on the concrete floor on the north side. The inscription on the tablet is the Buddhist creed stanza embossed on both sides of a seated figure of Avalokitesvara in Nāgarī characters of the 8th or 9th century A. D. The interior of the shrine yielded nothing except an irregularly shaped slab of stone inserted in the floor with an edging of brick, which cannot have been meant to hold an image. Possibly it was an Agnikunda as the digging brought to light heaps of ashes and charred wood both inside and outside the temple, possibly the remnants of fire sacrifices, performed by the adherents of the Brahmanical faith.

The Northern Area.

In the northern area Sir John Marshall's explorations have disclosed portions of three important monasteries for the residence of monks and nuns while others probably still lie buried as on the occasion of the visit of the Chinese pilgrim Hiuen Tsang, the Deer-Park was inhabited by as many as 1,500 monks. The monasteries so far excavated in this area were, as stated above, constructed in the late Kushāna period and continued in use with necessary repairs and improvements up to the time when the whole of the northern area was appropriated for the erection of the Dharmachakra-Jinavihāra which came to light quite near the surface of the existing ground. The following remarks about the last-mentioned edifice will show that it was, in reality, a temple or shrine and not a hospice as has hitherto been supposed. The three monasteries marked II, III and IV in the accompanying Plan lie at the depth of sixteen to eighteen feet below the present surface of the mound.

The Dharmachakra-Jinavihāra of Queen Kumāradevī of Kanauj. (So-called Monastery I.)

The building described in the previous editions of this handbook and the Archæological Survey Reports as Monastery I, is probably identical with the Shrine of the Lord of the Wheel of the Law, *i.e.*, Gautama Buddha, which according to a well-preserved inscription [D (*l*) 9] unearthed in 1907-08 was erected by Kumāradevī, the Buddhist queen of Govindachandra, king of Kanauj (A. D. 1114-1154). The part of the building so far exhumed already extends over an area exceeding 760 feet from east to west and consists of an imposing central block situated to the due north of the Main Shrine and preceded by two large open courts on the east, the area on the west side being occupied by a small shrine unearthed right at the edge of the site which was approached through a long subterranean passage (Sanskrit *surangā*). The entire precinct of the building was originally bounded by a solidly built brick wall 4′ 4″ thick, the greater part of which on the south side has been exposed and repaired. No attempt has yet been made to trace it on the north and west sides. It may have disappeared or portions of it may still be recovered.

The principal block of the monument has a curious plan which has not yet been noticed on any other Buddhist site. It comprises a square courtyard quite open on the west side but bounded on the other three sides by rooms whose floor was about six feet higher than that of the inner court. A reference to the accompanying Plan will show the foundation cells which have been completely explored on the east side but only partially on the north and south sides. The inner and outer walls of the plinth thus obtained are faced with neatly chiselled bricks lavishly adorned with moulded patterns which are best preserved in the south-east corner of the quadrangle. The actual apartments that stood on the top of these cells have entirely perished with the exception of a few remnants and we are left merely to guess what they were like. Assuming, however, that the walls of the superstructure followed the lines of the foundations, it is not difficult to reconstruct the general plan and design of the building especially as a great proportion of the stone-work* employed in the original construction has been reclaimed mainly from the inner court where it lay hidden beyond the reach of Babu Jagat Singh.

Relying on this evidence, we find that the inner court was surrounded on all the three sides, with which we are concerned, by a narrow hall or half open colonnade relieved at the corners by small square cells. To judge from a few base stones which exist in their original positions, the hall must have been supported on pillars and pilasters, half engaged in brick walls. It was about seven feet in depth and covered with a flat roof of horizontal slabs, some of which have been found in good condition. These slabs will be easily distinguished among the débris stacked on the north side of this building by broad lotus medallions carved on them.

From this colonnade jutted out double projections on the outside and single ones on the interior. The projection on the east side contains a flight of steps, now much ruined, an entrance chamber and guard rooms. The small square cells in the corners, as also those meant for the gate-keepers, have each, in addition to the brick walls, pilasters in the corners to provide extra support to the ceiling which appears to have been constructed on the principle of intersecting squares. The central covering slab (D*i* 117) of one of these cells is exhibited in the northern verandah of the Archæological Museum at Sārnāth. The purpose of the rooms on the other two sides of the quadrangle is not ascertainable. In all probability they were shrines for images, the portions of the colonnades in front, which projected several feet into the courtyard, doing duty as audience halls.

The inner courtyard was open to the sky. It was paved in concrete and plastered over with *kankar* lime. In the north-east corner of the court is a well with an inner diameter of five feet and a low parapet wall. It is of the same date as the temple, but the flights of steps by which the inner court is approached, and one of which has recently been repaired, were added at a somewhat later date.

The two extensive courts which, as stated above, precede the main temple building on the east side, measure 114′ and 290′ from east to west. A general view of them is obtainable from the entrance of the temple. The floor of the first court was paved with massive slabs of sandstone. Several fragments of this pavement were found in position but no sculptures of any kind have yet been traced upon it. These courts were

* These stones have been sorted and stacked in the area to the north of this building. They include cornice stones, drip-stones, door jambs, lintels, etc.

furnished with handsome entrances styled First Gateway and Second Gateway in the Plan of Excavations. The second was a more massive structure than the other. Both were flanked on the outside, with beautiful bastions and provided with well-constructed gatekeepers' chambers on the inside. The northern bastion of the First Gateway has survived in good condition. Of the Second Gateway only the heavy foundations remain, and as they go down to a considerable depth, namely, more than eight feet below the present ground level, they must have supported a lofty superstructure. The latter has wholly disappeared with the exception of a few remnants. It will be observed that both these gateways were constructed with the same kind of materials, namely, chiselled brick and stone and in the same style as the Dharmachakra-Jinavihāra to which they belong. As has been hinted above, it seems quite likely that another and larger gateway and one or more courts exist further to the east.

Shrine with Subterranean passage.

The entire area to the west of the principal block of the Dharmachakra-Jinavihāra, right up to the western limit of the site was included in this monument and enclosed by its outer boundary wall. The monument now brought to light in this area apart from the earlier monastery II to be referred to later on, is not a gateway or other conspicuous adjunct, but an underground structure. A part of it was exposed in 1907-08 and was then believed to be a drain for carrying off rain-water. It was completely cleared out in 1920 and turns out to be a subterranean passage, 160′ 9″ long, which led into a very small shrine.

The floor of the passage which is throughout paved with concrete is reached by a well-constructed flight of stone steps in very good preservation. At the foot of these steps there is a low entrance, the ceiling in front being so low that the votary must have had to crawl here evidently as a mark of reverence to the shrine referred to. Barring the entrance and a few feet of the passage adjoining it on both sides which are composed of stone, the rest of this subterranean passage is built of bricks measuring 9″×7″×1¾″, which is precisely the size of bricks used in the Dharmachakra-Jinavihāra. As was natural in an underground structure, the brick walls are chiselled, neatly laid and plastered on the inside, the masonry on the outside being coarse and uneven as it was not intended to meet the eye. The average width of the passage, which is 6 feet high, is 3′ 6″ throughout the length except for a small portion at the distance of 87 feet from the entrance where it widens out into a chamber 12′ 7″×6′ 10″ internally. This chamber had a separate flight of steps from above and has entrances at both ends. It is also evident that some kind of ventilators must have been inserted in the walls of this chamber. The greater part of the passage must, however, have remained in darkness even during the day and the little niches with corbelled tops occurring here and there in the walls must have been provided to hold earthen lamps. The roof of the passage consisted everywhere of flat slabs of stone, and in repairing it care has been taken to leave sufficient openings for the admission of light.

The shrine itself which measures roughly 8 feet square internally is ruined and only bases of its walls remain. In general design, it appears to have been analogous to the shrine of Vajravārāhī described above (p. 22). There might have been a sacred image in this shrine, but as noted above (p. 9) its main purpose would appear to have been to provide the monks with a solitary place for meditation.

This passage is perhaps the only example of a structural *suranga* of the pre-Muhammadan period so far known to us. Mughal forts often contain secret passages by which the occupants could escape on occasions of hostile invasion, etc. They are also frequently alluded to in Sanskrit literature and we readily recall the subterranean passage mentioned in the Ādiparva of the Mahābhārata in connection with the plot designed by Duryodhana against the lives of the Pāndava brothers.

No images have so far been found in the Dharmachakra-Jinavihāra except two female figures (Nos. B*f* 4 and 5 in the Museum) which were lying in front of the entrance to the principal block. These might be representations of the river goddesses Gangā and Yamunā*, though they are seated in an extraordinary posture and are not accompanied by their usual *vāhanas* (vehicles). It is, therefore, difficult to say to what deity the temple was dedicated. If, however, my identification of this building with the temple of Kumāradevī is correct, it must have enshrined an image of Vasudhārā, the goddess of abundance, as is clearly stated in the inscription referred to. The excavations at Sārnāth have yielded at least three fragmentary images of this goddess (B*f* 19, 20 and 21) of the same period as the temple and these might have belonged to it. It is also possible that the copper plate which Kumāradevī "had caused to be prepared in connection with the teaching of the Lord of the Wheel of the Law" was also installed in this temple.

In the above remarks I have assumed the identity of the building hitherto designated as monastery I with the Dharmachakra-Jinavihāra of Kumāradevī. The reasons that have led to this conclusion are briefly summarized here. In the first place it is plain that the building cannot be a monastery, (1) because in plan it differs essentially from the monasteries known to us on this and other Buddhist sites, which are invariably *chatuhsāla*, *i.e.*, surrounded with cells on all four sides, whereas the building being described is quite open on one side, (2) the structural arrangement is such as to afford little room for actual residential cells, (3) no other monastery known to us, is preceded by such extensive courts with elaborate gateways as occur in this building, and (4) builders of monasteries

* Mr. B. Bhattacharya in his *Buddhist Iconography* identifies these images as representations of Shadakshari Mahāvidyā.

seldom lavished such exuberant ornament on their works as is noticed on the various parts of this edifice. Moreover, the erection of this temple, under the name of Dharmachakra-Jinavihāra, is mentioned in the stone inscription of Kumāradevī [D (*l*) 9 in the Museum] which was unearthed by Sir John Marshall to the south of the second gateway of this building, but which originally must have been fixed at some conspicuous spot in the gateway itself. The building being described, on account of its decoration and boldness of design, well answers the high-sounding description of the *vihāra* built by Kumāradevī which was "an ornament to the earth" and "like to the palaces of gods"

There is, however, other proof of the correctness of this identification: The building is manifestly the work of a wealthy person or ruler as the expense and labour involved in levelling the vast area covered by it and its construction must have been enormous. The attachment of Kumāradevī to the Buddhist faith is known to us from a munificent grant of rent-free villages which, under her influence, her royal husband, who was himself an orthodox Hindu,* gave away for the benefit of the Buddhist Community residing at the Jetavana Monastery of Srāvastī. The same pious spirit must have been responsible for the foundation of this temple at Sārnāth. And, as it would have been derogatory to her high rank to build her temple with old material collected from the site, she ordered bricks of a special size of superior texture to be made for the purpose. Another reason why this temple should be ascribed to Kumāradevī, is that we are not aware of any other equally remarkable temple having been erected at Sārnāth about the period to which this temple belongs. Lastly, it is noteworthy that the building being described possesses broad enclosures and gateways resembling *gopurams* that form so striking a characteristic of the South-Indian style of architecture. Queen Kumāradevī came from Pīthi, *i.e.*, Pithāpuram, in the Godavari district and had her temple planned after a South-Indian model.

MONASTERY II.

Of the three monasteries which must be assigned to the late Kushāna or early Gupta epoch, Monastery II has been unearthed beneath the area to the west of the principal building of the Dharmachakra-Jinavihāra of Kumāradevī, its west wall forming the limit of the Deer-Park in that direction. The monument is in a very ruinous condition as it is nowhere standing to a height of more than three or four feet above the foundations and some parts have totally disappeared. In plan, the building is analogous to the monastery excavated by Major Kittoe, but the portion so far

* According to a Nepalese manuscript, king Govindachandra had another Buddhist wife named Vāsantadevi, though it is possible that Kumāradevi and Vāsantadevi were the names of one and the same lady.

laid bare comprises only nine chambers on the west side, parts of two chambers in the south-east corner, two rooms in the south wing and the greater part of the verandah wall on the south and west sides. In the verandah on the east side, we observe a temporary kitchen consisting of a low brick platform and two or three brick hearths, but the only utensils found here were plain earthen bowls and cooking pots. The inner open court of the monastery measures 90′ 10″ from east to west, and to judge from the parts exhumed, the external measurement of the building from side to side must have been about 165 feet. Of the chambers exposed in the west row, the sixth one from the south end is larger than the others and must have been the central cell on that side. None of the pillars, which supported the roof of the verandah all round the inner court, have survived in the portion of the building so far laid bare, but there is no doubt that they must have been in the same style and material as those of Monasteries III and IV. It may be observed that the base-stones of two of the pillars do exist at the south end of the west verandah wall.

It will be observed that this monastery is built upon the ruins of an earlier structure of the same character. A part of the brick pavement (now filled up) of this latter structure which was found in the trench alongside the south verandah wall of Monastery II, is six feet lower than the level of the latter. It is difficult as yet to ascertain the precise date of this earlier edifice; nor is it known whether still earlier structures exist underneath it.

Monastery III.

Monastery III is situated to the east of the temple of Kumāradevī and is the best preserved building of its kind laid bare at Sārnāth. It occupies a very low level, but a flight of stone steps has been recently provided near the south-west corner of the first outer court of the temple referred to. In plan, the building is similar to Monastery II described above. So far, four chambers on the south and the whole of the western range of cells together with a part of the inner courtyard and the verandah have been excavated. As the total number of cells on the west side is seven, there must have been twenty-four cells on the entire ground floor. The west outer wall which alone has so far been completely excavated measures 109′ 6″ long externally. The monastery appears to have had one or more upper storeys, and whatever means of access to them existed must be buried in the unexcavated portion of the building. The extant height of the walls averages 10 feet. The outer wall is 5′ 6″ thick on the west side and just over six feet on the south. The roof of the verandah, which is about 11 feet broad, was supported on free standing stone pillars at the outer edge and pilasters of the same material engaged in the front wall of the cells. The capitals, of which several specimens were found, are of the usual bracketed type. The visitor will observe that the wall crossing the west row of cells at the 5th chamber, several feet above its level belongs to the temple of Kumāradevī, and that the modern wall underneath it has been built merely for its protection.

The doorways of the cells are 6′ 7″ high and 4′ 2 broad. They were no doubt originally fitted with wooden doors which have disappeared. The wooden lintel of the entrance to cell No. 3 from the west end of the south row existed in a rotten condition and has been replaced by a new one. The carved brickwork above the lintel deserves notice. For better ventilation, most of the rooms would appear to have been furnished, high up in the outer walls, with window openings containing pierced stone screens. Two of these screens were unearthed in this monastery and may be seen in the Museum. The bricks in the interior walls of the cells are not chiselled, presumably because they were originally plastered over though no plaster was actually noticed in any of the cells excavated. The room to the east of the one just referred to is the entrance to the monastery. The eastern part of this room could not be excavated as it would have involved the removal of the first gateway of the temple of Kumāradevī, which stands immediately above it. The chamber at the back of the third cell on the south side was excavated down to a depth of 17 feet. It has no entrance of any kind, and can only have been some sort of a storage chamber or the foundation of an upper room which was entered from the first floor of the monastery.

The courtyard as well as the verandah floor and the floors of the cells are all paved with bricks, laid flat. The water from the courtyard was carried away by a covered drain in the south-west corner of the monastery. At the mouth of the drain a perforated stone is set up in vertical position to act as a trap. My excavations of 1922 revealed the fact that after leaving Monastery III, the drain ran in a westerly direction and is now hidden under a heavy accumulation of débris underneath the temple of Kumāradevī. A new drain similar in design to the original one has now been built with old bricks along the entire outer length of Monastery III.

In view of the absence of any datable antiques from these early monasteries, two small fragments of white marble reliefs, which were found last spring near the north-west outer corner of this monastery may be noticed here. Both the pieces appear to have belonged to representations of the attainment of spiritual wisdom by the Buddha and judging from their delicate technique they must have been carved about the late Kushāna period.

Monastery IV.

On returning to the higher ground we pass, on our right, the remnant of the First Gateway of the temple of Kumāradevī. We proceed towards the east until we reach Monastery IV discovered at a depth of some 15 feet below the ground level. The north-east corner of it, with two rooms on the east side and a part of the verandah on the east and north sides had been cleared in 1907-08 by Sir John Marshall. The only advance since made with the exploration of this monastery is the disclosure of four cells on the north side. The major part of the building still remains buried under the ground to the south of the south boundary wall of the temple of Kumāradevī, which crosses it some 10 feet above the level of its floor. Some of the stone columns which supported the open passage around the middle court were found lying flat on the floor and have now been re-erected. These columns are of the same general design as those of Monastery II, though they differ somewhat in detail. The verandah is 7′ 6″ to 7′ 10″ in width. The floor of the courtyard which is paved with bricks slopes slightly towards a drain in the north-east corner which carried off water from the interior of the building.

The large stone base lying behind the eastern rooms of this monastery on a somewhat higher level is the pedestal of a colossal Siva image of about 1000 A. D. [B (*h*) 1], which is now deposited in the Archæological Museum. Here it may be remarked that the image has nothing to do with the Buddhist Monastery we have been describing, as the latter must have been buried deep under the débris before the image was brought and put up where it has been found.

No other objects of interest were found on this part of the site except a number of iron household implements which belong approximately to the period when the monastery was destroyed.

Our route now takes us to the Second Gateway of the temple of Kumāradevī after which we make our way to the south where the lofty *stūpa* called Dhamekh rears its head towards the skies.

Major Kittoe unearthed a multitude of structures in the area around this edifice but they have all disappeared, and the monuments we now see to the north of the *stūpa* were excavated in 1907-08. They range in date from the late Gupta period to the 10th to 12th centuries A, D. These structures consist of *stūpas*, chapels, concrete floors, etc., and are built entirely of brick and plaster. Perhaps the most interesting of them all is the plinth of a *stūpa*, numbered 74 in the Plan of Excavations, now hidden under a later structure.

It was in this area that the beautifully engraved stone inscription of Queen Kumāradevī, referred to above, was found. In the same area were also discovered three well-preserved sculptures, 3′ 8″ to 4 feet in height, of about the 9th century A. D.,* which in that period might possibly have occupied three of the niches in the projecting faces of the Dhamekh *stūpa*.

* These are Nos. B(*c*) 2 and 35 and B (*d*) 8 of the Sārnāth Museum collection.

Dhamekh Stūpa.

The modern name Dhamekh is derived from a Sanskrit word *dharmekshā* meaning "the pondering of the Law". This *stūpa* is a solid structure rising to a height of 104 feet above the paved terrace of the Jaina temple adjoining it, or 143 feet if we include the foundations of the earlier *stūpa* which lie buried underneath it. The lower part of the basement is 93 feet in diameter and solidly built, the stones being secured together with iron cramps to a height of 37 feet above the terrace of the Jaina temple. The upper part of the structure is made of brick which was possibly originally faced with stone. This facing of stone, if it ever existed, must have been cut away by the workmen of Jagat Singh, referred to above, in 1794 A. D. It will be observed that the damage done to the lower part of the tower by Jagat Singh has recently been partly repaired by the Archæological Survey Department.

The basement is relieved on the outside by eight projecting faces each one of which has a large niche and pedestal which no doubt formerly held an image. As stated above, the three seated images (Bc 2 and 35 and B*d* 8) discovered in the area around this monument may possibly have adorned three of the niches in the 9th or 10th century A. D. Two of them represent Gautama Buddha at the moment of his enlightenment and as preaching his first sermon, while the third is an image of the Bodhisattva Avalokitesvara. The remaining five sculptures of this set have not yet been recovered, nor any of the earlier ones which were no doubt originally installed in these niches at the time of the construction of the existing structure. The precise character of those images is not known. They might have been seated effigies of the eight Buddhas* beginning with Vipasyin and ending with Maitreya, the future Buddha, or, what is equally possible, representations of the eight principal events of the historical Buddha's life.

The lower part of the basement is adorned with a broad belt of carved ornament consisting of an intricate geometric design with floral arabesques above and below it. The whole body of carving is singularly vigorous and exquisitely beautiful. On the evidence of style, it is attributable to the Gupta age and this, no doubt, is the date of the structure as we now see it. This conclusion is also amply borne out by the style and size of the bricks employed in the upper portion of the *stūpa*. In these circumstances, one is surprised to find Mr. Fergusson assigning the monument as late a date as the 11th century A. D., and Mr. Oertel denying its existence in the middle of the 7th century when Hiuen Tsang

* According to the Buddhist belief, innumerable Buddhas have appeared in past ages prior to Gautama Buddha or Sākyamuni. Among those that immediately preceded the Buddha of the present cycle, who was in reality a historical personage, three, seven and even twenty-three Buddhas are mentioned by name in the Buddhist texts. They are of course all believed to be mythical beings.

visited Sārnāth. The principal reason for such late dating of this structure appears to have been the discovery, in it, of an inscription of the 6th or 7th century A. D., containing the Buddhist creed. The slab (now in the Indian Museum at Calcutta) on which the epigraph is engraved was found in a well which General Cunningham dug into the building in 1835 A. D., at the depth of 10 feet from the top. It is evident, however, that the slab must have been inserted into the structure at some later date.

The unfinished condition of the carving on the *stūpa* seems to show that the building was never completed. It is likewise apparent that this is not the first structure on this spot. The foundations underneath it which General Cunningham found to be composed of very large bricks such as we find in the monuments of the third and second centuries B.C., must have belonged to an edifice of that period. What that monument was, we have at present no means of ascertaining. It was presumably a *stūpa* erected by the Emperor Asoka to commemorate some event in the life of Gautama Buddha. Hiuen Tsang, the Chinese traveller, must have seen the Dhamekh *stūpa* but unfortunately it is not yet possible to identify it with any of the monuments described by him.

MONASTERY V.

(So-called Hospital.)

This monastery was discovered a short distance to the west of the Dhamekh *stūpa* by Major Kittoe who identified it as a hospital because he found in it a large number of mortars and pestles. This view has been shown to be untenable by the recent excavations as it becomes evident that the monument was a monastery of the usual type. It dates from the 8th or 9th century A. D., but is built upon the remains of an earlier structure of the Gupta period. The upper building faces towards the west. The excavation has been partly filled in to prevent rain-water collecting in it.

Jaina Temple.

The Jaina temple spoken of above is a modern building situated to the south of the monument just described. It has a high enclosure wall and a spacious open court to the east abutting on the Dhamekh Stūpa. It is dedicated to the 11th Jaina patriarch Srī Amsanātha and was erected in 1824 A.D. There is nothing of archæological interest inside it.

Brahmanical Sculpture Shed.

The Brahmanical Sculpture Shed * to the west of the Jaina temple was erected by Mr. F. O. Oertel in 1905 for the temporary housing of the antiquities discovered by him at Sārnāth. All these antiquities have

* This is designated as the Old Sculpture Shed in the previous editions.

since been transferred to the new Archæological Museum. The sculptures now exhibited in this shed are Brahmanical and Jaina sculptures which do not originate from Sārnāth. The provenance of some of these sculptures has been ascertained from a volume of manuscript drawings prepared by Major Kittoe about 70 years ago.

All these sculptures are described in detail in my Catalogue of the Archæological Museum at Sārnāth. Here it is sufficient to introduce the visitor to a few of the exhibits which appear to be the most interesting of the lot. Perhaps the oldest sculpture in this shed is the incomplete stone image (G 2; ht. 3′ 7½″) of the river goddess Yamunā standing opposite the visitor as he enters the hall. The Goddess is standing, as usual, on her vehicle the tortoise and is attended by a number of votaries one of whom holds an umbrella over her head. Judging from the style of carving, the statue must be assigned to the Gupta period. It is believed to have been brought from Bhitari in the Ghazipur District, and not from Bhitargaon as wrongly stated in the *Catalogue*, page 314. Another sculpture (ht. 2′ 2″; w. 1′ 11″) that dates from about the same period is G 33. It presumably depicts a scene from the Hindu epic, the Rāmāyana, namely, the construction, by Rāma's monkey comrade Nīla, of the bridge at Rāmesvaram* over which he passed to Lanka with his army. In the upper portion of the composition we notice a headless figure of Rāma who holds his bow in his left hand, and is seated on a rock. He is attended by his younger brother Lakshmana, while the figures in front of him are presumably Sugrīva and Hanuman. The rest of the sculpture is occupied by a representation of the sea distinguished by figures of a fish, a crocodile, a conch shell, etc., and of the monkey warriors who are carrying stones for the building of the bridge.

Among the mediæval sculptures in the shed we notice especially the lintel (G 38), 8′ 3″ wide, bearing figures of the nine planets, beginning with the sun at the extremity of the left hand sunken panel and ending with the demons Rāhu and Ketu at the end of the other panel. Of the three projections, one in the middle, and one at each end of the lintel, the former contains a figure of Srī, the goddess of wealth. The temple to which the lintel belonged must, therefore, have been dedicated to a Vaishnava deity. The miniature spire shrines of stone placed at the corners of the compound wall are Brahmanical votive shrines, none of which are earlier than the late mediæval period.

Among the Jaina sculptures preserved in this shed, the visitor's attention may particularly be directed to No. G61, bearing images of four of the Jaina patriarchs Mahāvīra, Ādinātha, Sāntinātha and Ajitanātha and to No. 62 which represents the eleven th Jina Srī Amsanātha.

* This interpretation is more plausible than the one tentatively offered in my Catalogue of the Museum of Archæology at Sārnāth.

The Sārnāth Museum of Archæology.

The Sārnāth Museum of Archæology stands on the opposite side of the road as we descend from the plateau representing the ancient Deer-Park. The construction of this building was proposed by Sir John Marshall soon after the excavations described above had been taken in hand in 1904-05. The necessary designs were prepared by Mr. James Ransome, then Consulting Architect to the Government of India, who appropriately selected for his model the usual type of the ancient monastery, several examples of which have been excavated at Sārnāth. The part of the building so far erected represents less than a half of the quadrangle of which the Buddhist convent consists; the rest of the building will be completed when more space becomes necessary. A detailed catalogue of the antiquities preserved in the Museum was prepared by the author of this hand-book in 1912 but this publication has been out of print for several years.

The total number of antiquities so far recovered from the Buddhist ruins of Sārnāth is about 4,000. These collections consist of sculptures, bas-reliefs, fragments of railings, pottery vessels, terracotta figurines, seals and impressions of seals and stone inscriptions, and with the exception of a few specimens to be noticed in their proper places all pertain to the Buddhist religion. They cover a period of some 1,500 years, *i.e.*, from the 3rd century B. C. to the end of the 12th century A. D. All these objects were hitherto displayed in four out of the eight rooms of the museum building, and there was much confusion and congestion. In 1929-30 the collections were overhauled and only the most striking and typical specimens have been retained and re-arranged in a chronological order (Pl. III). Duplicates and specimens of less importance have been transferred to Room 4 in the north wing of the Museum and to two other rooms and an open platform at the back of the main building. Visitors desirous of viewing these latter specimens are requested to apply to the Custodian of the Museum. The paragraphs that follow are intended to supply only such information about the exhibits in the main building as is considered necessary for the understanding of the collections.

Room 1 or the Central Hall in the East Wing contains some of the largest and finest exhibits in this Museum. The well-preserved monument standing in the centre of the room is the capital (Plate IV) of the Asoka pillar described above. It is just 7 feet high and consists of a Persepolitan bell-shaped lower member surmounted by four lions standing back to back, the middle portion or abacus above the fluted bell being adorned with the figures of a lion, an elephant, a bull and a horse. Speaking of the technique of these figures and the crowning lions, Sir John Marshall remarks that " they are wonderfully vigorous and true to nature and treated with that simplicity and reserve which is the keynote of all great masterpieces of plastic art. India certainly has produced no other sculpture equal to them". The late Dr. Bloch was of the opinion that the four figures on the abacus symbolized the goddess Durgā, Indra, Siva and Sūrya, whose vehicles these animals respectively are and that they were carved upon this capital to signify the subordination of these Brahmanical deities to Gautama Buddha and his law. Dr. Vogel identified these figures as representations of the four noble beasts (Mahājāneya) of the Buddhists, used merely as ornamental motifs. I owe the correct explanation of these reliefs to a Burmese Pāli scholar whom I had the pleasure of showing round the Museum some years ago. This is that the drum with the four animals is intended to represent the Anotatta lake of the Buddhist texts, in which the Buddha used to bathe. It was also with the water of this lake that his mother Mahāmāyā was bathed before her conception. The lake, as described and illustrated in a Buddhist manuscript on palm leaves in Burmese characters, had four mouths, guarded by these very animals, namely, by the lion on the east, the elephant on the south, etc. I have no doubt that in its original position on the top of the Asoka pillar, this capital must have been oriented in the same manner, so that the animals faced their respective directions. It is interesting to note that the Archæological Section of the Central Museum at Lahore contains a small square terracotta plaque showing a circular depression in the middle surrounded by the same four animals, arranged in the same order. This plaque is, to my mind, a true representation of the Anotatta lake and must have been used for worship. The only point of difference between this tablet and the relief on the Asoka capital is that, whereas the four animals on the latter are separated by representations of the Buddhist Wheel of the Law (*dharmachakra*), the intervening symbols on the terracotta tablet in the Lahore Museum are a conch, a bowl containing the hair of the Buddha (Pāli *chūlāmaho*), the Wheel of the Law and the *triratna* (three jewel) symbol.

The crowning feature of the capital was a large wheel carved in the round chosen by the Emperor Asoka and his artists in reference to the traditional comparison of the Buddhist doctrine to that symbol. Four fragments of the periphery and three pieces of the spokes of this wheel were recovered by Mr. Oertel in 1904-5 and are shown in the lowest shelf of the wall-case in the middle of the north wall of this room.

In the northern half of this hall are displayed specimens of the Sunga and Kushāna periods (Cir. 180 B. C. to 200 A. D.). The colossal standing statue in red sandstone, B(*a*) 1, represents Gautama Buddha in the state of Bodhisattva, *i.e.*, before he attained enlightenment or became a Buddha in the 36th year of his life at Gaya. This statue was originally sheltered by a large stone umbrella. The greater part of the shaft of this umbrella is fixed in the pedestal behind the statue; but the top which is profusely sculptured in the form of a full blown lotus with fabulous beasts and sacred symbols has had to be set up separately near the north-east corner of the hall. It is put together from ten pieces and is therefore unfit for restoration upon its shaft. From inscriptions engraved, one in front of the base and another on the back of this statue and a third one on its octagonal umbrella post, we learn that the statue and the umbrella were donated by a Buddhist monk of Mathurā named Bala and erected at Benares at the place where Lord Buddha used to walk for exercise (*chamkama*) in the third regnal year of the Kushāna king Kānishka. This *chamkama* of the Buddha has not yet been identified, but that a structure of this kind, resembling the one at Bodh Gaya which had a roof supported on pillars with vase-shaped bases, did exist at Sārnāth is evidenced by a similar base, D(*g*)25, which has been found on this site and is exhibited a few feet from the statue being described.

The statue B(*a*)2 with the lower part of its umbrella post set up by its side immediately behind the red stone statue of the friar Bala was carved at Sārnāth and in Chunār stone and is a faithful copy of it. The figure of the lion between the feet is, here, as in the original, meant to emphasise the epithet, " Lion of the Sākya race ", by which the Buddha is frequently referred to in the Buddhist texts. The red colouring imparted to this statue must evidently have been due to a desire on the part of the Sārnāth sculptor to make his copy resemble the original in every way possible. A statue which may be assumed to mark the transition from the Kushāna to the Gupta period is that with a scalloped halo, B(*b*)1, which may be assigned to the 3rd century A. D. All these three statues are represented in what is known in Buddhist texts as the *abhayamudrā* or the posture of granting security. The other attitudes or *mudrās* in which Buddha images are generally represented are :—the gift-bestowing attitude (*varamudrā*) in which the right arm is stretched down with the palm of the hand turned outwards ; the attitude of meditation (*dhyānamudrā*) expressed by the hands resting in the lap one over the other ; the earth-touching attitude (*bhūmisparśamudrā*) symbolising the moment of the enlightenment of the Great Man, in which the right hand of the image points down towards the Earth whom he called up to be his witness ; and the attitude of preaching or " turning the Wheel-of-the-Law " in which the hands of the image are so held in front of the breast that the thumb and the forefinger of the right hand touch the middle or the forefinger of the left hand.

Buddhist *stūpas*, umbrellas at their tops, temples and sacred trees were often surrounded by stone railings. Two sides of such a railing have been reconstructed to the north and north-west of the colossal statue from Mathurā with ten out of 12 rail posts, D(*a*)1 to D(*a*)12, which belonged to one and the same railing. The bevelled coping, D(*a*)40, on the western row bears a relief in which a *stūpa*, whose umbrella and streamers alone have survived, is being worshipped by a lady followed by a row of four animals, elephants alternating with buffaloes. The posts are also decorated with reliefs: one of them, D(*a*)7, shows on one face a *stūpa*, a *gandhakuṭī* surrounded by a railing and preceded by two (*torana*) gateways, winged lions facing in opposite directions, and a vase with palmettes; and on the other a pillar supporting the Wheel-of-the-Law (*dharmachakra*), which rests upon a trident made up of two crocodiles. The trident or *triratna* symbol stands for the Buddha, the Buddhist Law (*Dharma*) and the Buddhist Community (*Sangha*). D(*a*)1 and D(*a*)11 have similar motiffs and others including the *pīpal* tree hung with garlands, vases with acanthus leaves and lotus buds.

Part of another railing has been reconstructed against the north wall. It is more ancient than the one just described, and a well preserved inscription upon its coping, D(*a*)39, records that this stone was dedicated by a nun named Saṃvahikā. Two other posts, D(*a*)13 and D(*a*)15, which belonged to the same railing have been set up on a separate pedestal at the same corner of the room; one of these posts was in the Gupta period re-employed as a lamp-post in the Mūlagandhakuṭī.

The well-carved capital, D(*g*)4, standing between the Asoka capital and the Bodhisattva image of friar Bala, B(*a*)1, dates from the Sunga period (Cir. 100 B. C.); the end of a *torana* lintel, D(*h*)1, a few feet west of it, is somewhat later. The fragment, D(*a*)42, shows four *triratnas* around the Wheel-of-the-Law. Worth noticing is also the well-carved lintel, C(*b*)9, which shows the *stūpa* of Rāmagrāma, one of the eight in which the cremated corporeal remains of the Buddha were enshrined after his *parinirvāna* at Kusanagara (modern Kasia, District Gorakhpur). According to a Buddhist legend this *stūpa* was protected by *nāgas* and consequently not opened by Asoka.

The wall-case set against the north wall of the Central Hall contains some valuable objects. In the top shelf are fragments of abaci of capitals of sandstone bearing the same high polish as the pillars of Asoka and therefore assignable to the same early period. Several of these bear Brāhmī inscriptions recording gifts of private donors including those from Ujjayinī (modern Ujjain) and Pātaliputra (modern Patna). At least one of these abaci retains traces of the Persepolitan bell beneath it, showing that in all probability it formed part of a smaller pillar of the same type as the Asoka pillar described above. At what particular spot in the Deer-Park these pillars stood and what purpose they served remains a mystery. The second shelf from the top contains portrait heads of the 2nd century B. C.:—one, W 4, has a curled moustache and another, W 1, a wreath of flowers round its battlemented head-dress. All these heads are carved in the round and have been polished like the Asoka monuments though the polish is of an inferior quality. One other head, B 1, has a knot on the top of the skull, the rest of the head being shaven clean. Another noteworthy piece in this shelf is a fragmentary kneeling female figure also cut in the round, 210 W. The upper part of the body is left bare; the girdle round the waist consists of three strings of beads. To the same period, *i.e.*, the Sunga period, belong two female heads, 221 W and 229 W, at the right end of the shelf. Their elaborate head-dresses bedecked with beads recall the style of the Bharhut figures.

The objects in the shelf next below include seven large begging bowls of fine black and brown clay. The next lower shelf contains the heads of animals, a headless female chauri-bearer, a remarkable fragment, C(*b*)28, showing in a very realistic manner a woman absorbed in grief, her face buried in her arms upon her knees. Fragments, W 12-16, represent geese and a parrot which no doubt adorned abaci of capitals of Asoka pillars like those of the pillars at Rāmpurvā and Lauria Nandangadh in the Champaran District.

Among the antiquities in the lowest shelf of this wall-case is a fragment showing the crossed legs, B(*a*)5, of one of the red sandstone statues which were imported from Mathurā in the Kushāna period and supplied models for the sculptors of Benares. B(*a*)4 also belonged either to the same statue or another one from the same manufactory. This fragment shows a branch of the *pīpal* tree and belonged no doubt to a representation of the 'temptation' scene. The left hand portion of this shelf contains four fragments of the wheel which originally crowned the capital of the Asoka pillar and which, to judge from the pieces that fit together, must have had 32 spokes; there are also in this shelf a few fragments of the Asoka pillar containing portions of the first four or five lines of the edict.

The sculptures in the southern half of the Central Hall belong to the Gupta period (Circa 350—650 A. D.). The only exception is the colossal statue, B(*a*)3, with its well preserved shaft standing behind it, which represents Gautama Buddha before his enlightenment like the statues, B(*a*)1 and B(*a*)2, described above. Of the rest, nine standing figures on pedestals along the east wall and at the south-east corner are of Buddha in the *abhayamudrā*. One of them, B(*b*)4, has a particularly large halo. Three others, 39E, 40E and 22E, bear important inscriptions in Gupta characters. The first two were dedicated by a monk named Abhayamitra in the year 154 of the Gupta era (A. D. 473-474) and the third, 22E, also by the same monk, but in the year 157 (A. D. 476-477) in the reign of Buddhagupta. These inscriptions have thrown valuable light on the chronology of the Imperial Gupta kings. The space between the doorways leading into the Gupta gallery and the verandah is occupied by the well-known sculpture representing the Buddha preaching, B(*b*) 181 (Plate V), circa 5th century A. D. Observe the elaborately carved halo with two *devas* bringing presents of flowers, the five first disciples and the donatrix with her child. and the Wheel-of-the-Law between them, which are portrayed upon the base of the image. About a century later is the large figure in high relief, B(*b*) 175, representing the Buddha's enlightenment, when, seated upon the *vajrāsana* at Bodh Gaya, he defeated the Evil One and reached supreme spiritual wisdom. The mutilated figure beneath the right hand represents the Earth goddess, whom he had summoned to be the witness of his former meritorious acts, and the figure in sportive attitude at the other end of the base one of the three daughters of Māra, who tried to seduce the Great Man. The figure next to this, B(*b*) 174, is a better preserved representation of this event. Note the figure of the Dhyāni Buddha Amoghasiddhi in the Buddha's head-dress. The statue in reddish sandstone, B(*d*)2, with high head-dress and long locks hanging over the shoulders is presumably Maitreya, Messiah of the Buddhists, who will be born at Kedumati and will become Buddha under a Nāga tree, 5,000 years after the passing of the Sākyamuni Buddha. Another noteworthy figure is the female statuette, B(*f*)1, which presumably represents one of the aspects of the Buddhist goddess Tārā and is an excellent illustration of the exaggerated points of personal beauty as conceived by the mediæval poets, Kālidāsa, etc. Note also the elaborate jewellery with which the figure is bedecked. The next figure which appears to have remained unfinished, represents Vajrapāni, holding a thunderbolt (*vajra*) with his right hand and a bell in the left. His spiritual preceptor Amitābha appears in his high-peaked crown. B(*d*)1 is one of the earliest and finest representations of Lokanātha. Note here the two *sūchīmukha pretas* (emaciated and tantalised spirits) with hands stretched up to receive drops of nectar trickling down the right hand of the deity. The inscription on the base of the statue declares that this image was the gift of the district officer Suyāttra and contains the pious wish that the merit accruing from this gift may help the attainment of supreme knowledge by all sentient beings. The next figure, B(*d*)6 (Plate VI), is Siddhaikavīra, one of the many forms of the Bodhisattva Manjusrī. The figure, B(*d*)3, adjoining the entrance door holding a bowl between his hands and with a figure of Amitābha on his head has been identified as Nīlakantha, one of the many varieties of the Bodhisattva Lokesvara.

Room 2 or Gupta Room.—The long gallery to the south of the Central Hall is reserved for bas-reliefs and other antiquities of the Gupta period (Cir. 350-650 A.D.). The sculptures in this collection depict one or other of the four or eight principal events of the life of the Buddha. The former set is depicted by the Stele No. C (*a*) 1, standing at the left end of the long masonry platform along the east wall. This relief is divided up into four sections which from the bottom upwards represent :—(1) The birth of prince Siddhārtha or Gautama Buddha. Here we see the Great man's mother Mahāmāyā standing under a *sāl* tree with her sister Prajāpati on her left. To her right is the god Indra who received the child on his birth. At the right end of the panel is the new-born baby with two serpent deities, Nāgas Nanda and Upananda, giving him a bath. (2) The 'temptation' of the Bodhisattva Gautama by Māra, the Evil One, before his attainment of spiritual wisdom at Gaya : a complete representation of the event. Here we see the Bodhisattva seated in the Earth-touching attitude under a *pīpal* tree. The Evil One holding his bow and arrow and attended by his standard-bearer stands to the right of the Master and two of his daughters Rati (Lust) and Prīti (Pleasure) to his left. The third daughter is seen in front of the throne. Note also two of Māra's devils at the upper corners. One of them is brandishing his sword with his right hand and holding a snake in his left ; the other has raised his left finger in a threatening attitude. The figure seated in front of the standard bearer supporting his head upon his left hand is the Evil One, foiled in his purpose. (3) The first sermon at the Deer-Park. Note Maitreya, the future Buddha, to the right and Padmapāni holding a full-blown lotus to the left of the Teacher. Observe also the wheel, the pair of deer, the five first disciples and the donor of the sculpture in front of the base. (4) The *parinirvāna* or the Great Decease. The Buddha is lying on his right side facing the spectator with four mourners in front of his couch ; the fifth figure with its back turned towards the spectator being the recluse Subhadra of Kusinagara (modern Kasia in the Gorakhpur District). the last convert of the Buddha. The figure at the feet of the Buddha represents his great disciple Mahākāsyapa of Rājagriha, who adored the Master's feet immediately before the cremation of his body. In the figure near the Buddha's head, holding a fan, we recognize the elder Upavāna. The four figures with their hands raised in grief are celestial mourners and the female figures, issuing from the trees at either end of the panel, the tree-spirits engaged in showering flowers. Note the *stūpa* at the top of the stele.

The same four events are depicted in the four corner panels of Stele C (*a*) 3 standing next to the one just described. Of the remaining four events depicted on this slab, that marked (*e*) represents the descent of the Buddha at Sankāsya (modern Sankassa, District Farrukhabad) from the heaven of the thirty-three to which he had risen from Srāvastī to expound the *abhidharma* to his deceased mother Māyā. While the Master was about to descend to the earth, Sakra or Indra ordered Visvakarman to construct a triple ladder, the foot of which was put in the town of Sankāsya. Flanked by Brahmā on the right and by Sakra on the left the Buddha descended. The ladder is not represented in the relief but Brahmā holding his *kamandalu* in his left hand and Indra holding an umbrella over the head of the Great Man are easily recognised. The panel marked (*f*) portrays the miracle of Srāvastī which consisted in the Buddha being seen preaching at the same time in different places emitting fire and water simultaneously from his body. Thus suspended in the air, the Master preached and defeated his Jaina opponent. The figure at the left lower corner represents this heretical teacher and the corresponding figure on the opposite side kneeling in reverence, the King Prasenajit. The panel marked (*c*) illustrates the presentation of honey to the Buddha by a monkey in the Pārileyyaka forest near Kausāmbī, to which the Great Man had retired for some time in his ninth retreat owing to the disorderly behaviour of his disciples. After this meritorious act, the monkey is stated to have committed suicide by throwing himself into a well and to have been reborn as a celestial being. This event is illustrated at the right end of the panel. The panel (*d*) alongside of the one described, depicts the subjugation of the infuriated elephant Nālagiri or Ratnapāla, which at the instigation of the Buddha's jealous cousin, Devadatta, had been let loose in order that it might kill the Great Man when he was on his way to the house of a Brāhmana who had invited him and his 500 disciples to a meal. The beast was, of course, readily subdued and is seen kneeling at the Buddha's feet in submission. The figure to the left of the Buddha probably represents Ānanda, the only one out of his party who remained with him when all the others had fled.

The third stele, C (*a*) 2 (Plate VII), of this kind is an excellent specimen of early Gupta art and though it is incomplete, the reliefs that have survived upon it are in excellent preservation. Two of the events portrayed on this slab are not found in the two stelae described above. One of these is the dream of Māyādevī when she perceived a white elephant descending from the heaven and entering her person. This was interpreted by soothsayers as meaning that a Great Man would be born to her. The other event is the great Renunciation, when the prince riding on his favourite horse Kanthaka and attended by his groom Chhandaka left his palace at the dead of night in quest of divine wisdom. Behind the horse is seen the prince cutting off his hair with his sword and higher up a fairy flying with the hair in a bowl to the heaven of the thirty-three gods where it was enshrined in a *chaitya*.

C (*a*) 5 and the next three sculptures, B20, B (*b*) 180 and B (*c*) 45 represent the Srāvastī miracle. These are followed by a row of standing Buddhas in the *abhayamudrā*. The unnumbered sculpture at the south end of the east wall shows the Hindu god Bhairava seated, bowl in right hand, *trisūla* (trident) in left hand and a skull between a pair of hands in the crown ; a wild animal's tooth forms the pendant of the god's necklace. This figure was found in the little shrine at the south-east corner of the fore-court of the Main Shrine which at a later date was reappropriated to Brahmanical worship.

The wall-case at the middle of the east wall contains carved bricks of the Gupta period (Cir. 350-650 A.D.) in the topmost shelf and stone and stucco heads of Buddhas and Bodhisattvas in the second sheu. The much defaced terracotta plaque at the right end of the fourth shelf shows the Srāvastī miracle and that [F (*a*) 4] at the opposite end the 'temptation' scene. Here observe the half-bodied Earth-goddess emerging from the earth with a treasure vase (*dhanaghata*) between her hands. The lowest shelf contains brick capitals with lotus and other patterns cut into them, such as are frequently noticed on the drums of *stūpas*. The terracotta plaque in the middle of the lowest shelf, F (*a*) 2, shows the Srāvastī miracle. Here notice the stem of the lotus upon which the Buddha is seated supported by Nāgas. To the left of the relief is the Jaina patriarch with an attendant holding an umbrella over his head

Of the four table cases in the centre of the room the one at the north end contains several Buddha statuettes of bronze, a small copper plate containing the Buddhist creed formula (Dharmaparyāya), fragments of copper bangles, a spouted jug of copper and a vase with the top fitted with a hinge.

Pillars Nos. D (*f*) 9, D (*f*) 3 and D (*f*) 10 standing between the table cases are typical specimens of the Gupta period. Some of the Buddha and Bodhisattva heads in the last show-case are also worth noticing ; also some very well carved hands, which still retain their red colour. Note, too, in this show-case the inscription on the umbrella fragment, D (*c*) 11, containing the Four Noble Truths (p. 2 *supra*), and inscribed pedestals of images.

The double masonry bench along the west wall of this gallery containing pedestals, some with the feet of the images still remaining upon them and with inscriptions in front. The upper step bears several well decorated lintels of doorways.

Room 3 in the south wing.—The colossal statue in high relief standing against the east wall represents Govardhanadhara or Krishna holding up the Govardhana hill at Mathurā. This miracle was performed to shelter the cow-herds from the heavy rain which Indra, offended by the loss of his offerings, had sent down to destroy the followers of Krishna. The missing portions of this sculpture have not yet been found. Although both the arms are broken off, the left hand is clearly seen applied to the projecting portion at the top of the sculpture which represents the hill. Observe the boar's or tiger's teeth as pendants of the necklace. This sculpture was discovered in the city of Benares, but in view of its close affinities with the Gupta sculptures unearthed at Sārnāth, it has been brought over and placed in the Sārnāth Museum.

The rest of this room is occupied by sculptures and architectural members of the mediæval period (Cir. 600-1200 A.D.). Along the south wall, notice especially B (*c*) 2, ' temptation '; B (*c*) 36 showing

Buddha preaching, and B (*c*)1 with an important inscription of two Pāla brothers who, under the orders of Mahīpāla, King of Bengal, carried out extensive works of repair and restoration at Sārnāth in Vikrama Samvat 1083 (A. D. 1026), *vide* p. 6 above. C (*a*) 8 shows the presentation of honey by the monkey. This sculpture is made of blue granite of which all Magadhan sculptures are made and must have been imported from Gaya. B (*d*) 8 shows the Bodhisattva Avalokitesvara. In the wall case at the middle of the south wall are a number of miniature clay *stūpas* (*dharmasarīras*) containing the Buddhist creed formula ; fragments of monk's bottles ; terracotta figurines ; terracotta tablets inscribed with Buddhist *sūtras* in very minute letters ; tablets with rows of *stūpas* above and the Buddhist creed below. There are also a few seal-dies or matrices (F *d* 1-3), in which the legend is engraved in countersunk reversed characters. Some of the sealings or impressions must originally have been attached to letters or parcels, and these are easily distinguished from the marks of the string with which the articles were first fastened. The practice of sealing letters and parcels in this way is frequently alluded to in ancient Sanskrit literature and the excavations carried out by the Archæological Department at this and other sites have brought to light the name-seals of princes, ministers, other State officials, private individuals, etc. The majority of the seal impressions preserved in this wall case are, however, votive tablets which were presented by pilgrims at the various Buddhist shrines at Sārnāth. Such tablets appear also to have been taken away by pious visitors as souvenirs of their pilgrimage to sacred places. The sealings, Nos. F *d* 4-8, which date from the 6th or 7th century A.D. were presented at the Principal Shrine of the Blessed One (Sanskrit Mūlagandhakuṭī). This shrine must originally have been a small hut in which the Buddha resided, and been converted afterwards into a temple. The rest of these tablets contain the well-known Buddhist formula referred to above, which was recited by the fifth disciple of the Buddha, named Asvajit, to Upatissa, who afterwards became known as Sāriputta, one of the two principal disciples of the Master. Upatissa had questioned Asvajit as to who was his teacher and whose doctrine he approved and he uttered this statement in reply :—

> " Of all the phenomena sprung from a cause,
> The Buddha the cause has told,
> And, he tells too how each shall come to its end,
> Such alone is the word of the Sage."

The same formula is reproduced in several unbaked sealings in the lowest shelf, which were found in *stūpa* No. 40 to the north-east of the Main Shrine.

Next to the wall case, note the figures of Mārichi, B (*f*) 24 and B (*f*) 23, with her car drawn by seven pigs, a large standing Tārā, B (*f*) 2, opposite the entrance. B (*e*) 1 shows Kuvera, the Buddhist God of Wealth, and his consort Hāriti; B (*e*) 6, three-seated figures representing Shadakshara Lokesvara, one of the forms of the Bodhisattva Avalokitesvara. The male figure to his proper right shows Manidhara and the female to his left-Shadaksharī Mahāvidyā, symbolizing the six-syllabled *Mantra,* Om Manipadme Hum. In the second wall-case in this room note the small but well preserved and well carved white lime-stone pláque, K16, showing Simhanāda Lokesvara. A fragment of another similar plaque represents the birth scene, from which only half the figure of Māyā is preserved, then the first sermon and above this, the miracle of Rājagriha, *i.e.*, the subduing of the elephant Nālagiri. The death scene occupies the top of the fragment. Note also in this case the pottery vessels including spouted jars, *gharas*, *handis*. A 12 represents Brahmā with his *hamsa* or goose behind him. He holds the sacrificial ladle and the Veda in the upper hands. D (*h*) 3 and D (*h*) 4 at the end of the walls represent leogryphs ridden by warriors. The colossal image B (*h*) 1 standing against the west wall of this room is the Hindu god Mahādeva spearing the demon Tripura with his *trisūla*. Of the inscription slabs set against the north wall note the one, D (*l*) 9, which records the construction of the Dharmachakra-Jinavihāra temple of Queen Kumāradevī (p. 28 above).

The north entrance of this room opens into a verandah in which are arranged on masonry platforms architectural stones of sorts, door-lintels, sculptured friezes, etc. The most interesting of these is the large lintel [D (*d*) 1; length 16′] of a doorway of the Gupta period, fourth or fifth century A. D. The face of the sculpture is divided into six panels. The panels at the ends of the lintel contain representations of Kubera, the Buddhist God of Wealth. The remaining four panels illustrate a legend connected with one of the previous existences of the Buddha in which he was tortured to death by order of a cruel king of Benares, named Kalābū, for preaching the virtues of patience to his dancing girls. The two panels in the middle of the lintel show them engaged in a musical performance apparently to lull the king to sleep. The king himself is absent. In the second panel from the right we see the same girls listening to the ascetic while the corresponding panel at the other end shows the torture of the sage by an executioner who is cutting off his right hand with a sword. The two females who try to restrain the executioner from the cruel act must be two of the courtesans.

M2DGA—3,000—29.9.33—GIPS

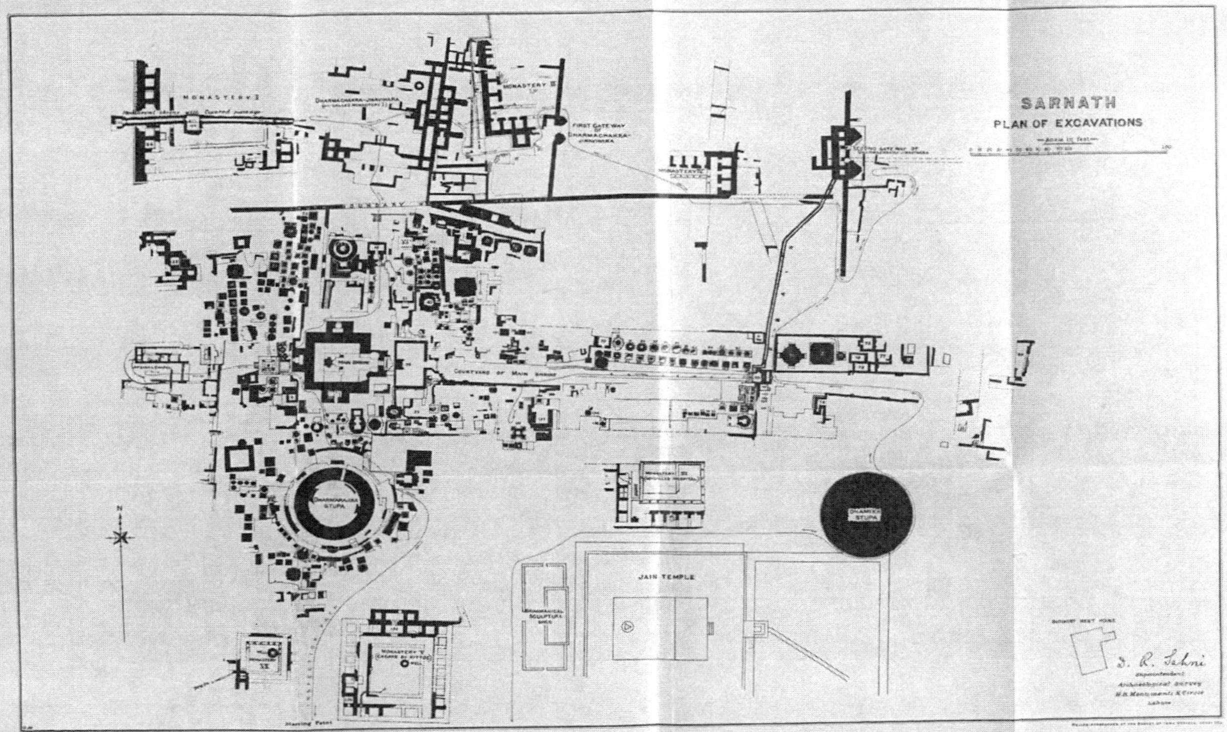
SARNATH
PLAN OF EXCAVATIONS
MONASTERY I
MONASTERY II
FIRST GATE WAY OF DHARMACHAKRA-JINVIHARA
COURTYARD OF MAIN SHRINE
DHARMARAJIKA STUPA
DHAMEKH STUPA
JAIN TEMPLE
BRAHMANICAL SCULPTURE SHED
N
D. R. Sahni
Archaeological Survey

SPECIMEN OF CARVING ON DHAMEKH STUPA.

Plate III.

View in Room 1 or Central Hall after re-arrangement.

LION. CAPITAL.

B (b) 181. BUDDHA PREACHING HIS FIRST SERMON.

B (*d*) 6. BODHISATTVA MANJUSRI (?).

C(a) 2. STELE REPRESENTING EVENTS FROM THE BUDDHA'S LIFE.